LOST & FOUND

A MEMOIR AND COMPASS FOR ANYONE IN SEARCH
OF MORE LOVE, HAPPINESS, AND MEANING

ALLA POLSKY

The events and conversations in this book have been chronicled to the best of the author's ability, although some names and details have been changed to protect the privacy of individuals.

Copyright © 2023 by Alla Polsky

All rights reserved. No part of this book may be reproduced or used in any manner without written permission of the copyright owner, except for the use of quotations in a book review.

First paperback edition August 2023

Cover Photography by Carlos Marcús

ISBN 979-8-9876160-1-7 (Paperback)

ISBN 979-8-9876160-0-0 (E-book)

Published by Alla Gonopolsky

For Babushka, in whom I found strength.

For Mumsie, in whom I found comfort.

For Herb, in whom I found my heart.

For you, dear reader, in whom I found my voice.

Contents

Introduction & Confession 1

PART I: FINDING LOVE

1. I Was Single For A Whole Darn Decade 10
2. Synchronicity Does Not Mean It's Fate 24
3. Manifesting Doesn't Need Details 31
4. Self-Love Doesn't Make You A Narcissist 42
5. Empaths Are Getting Bad Advice 52

PART II: FINDING PURPOSE

6. A One-Step Guide To Finding Yourself 60
7. A Reason You Don't Know Your Purpose Yet 65
8. A Message From Your Intuition 73
9. A School For Getting Out Of Your Own Way 88

PART III: FINDING COURAGE

10. Joining The Cult Of Scuba Diving 102
11. Nearly Dying While Scuba Diving 111
12. Nearly Ready To Teach Yoga 117

| 13. | Fully Ready To Travel Alone | 126 |

PART IV: FINDING HAPPINESS

14.	Can You Actually Travel Yourself Happy?	138
15.	Not Getting Your Way Is A Gift From The Future	147
16.	A Gift From A Stranger In My Past	153
17.	Actually Useful Ways To Be Unhappy	159
18.	Actually Useful Happiness Research Findings	176

PART V: FINDING ENLIGHTENMENT

19.	The Most Boring Spiritual Awakening Ever	188
20.	The First Step To Enlightenment	200
21.	The Perks Of Dating A Meditation Teacher	211
22.	My Dead Grandma Helps Me Lucid Dream	219
23.	My Living Boyfriend Hypnotizes Me	226

SECRET BONUS CHAPTER

| 24. | Timeless Wisdom From My Babushka | 240 |

Afterword	247
Acknowledgements	252
Notes	253

Introduction & Confession

This was supposed to be a travel book.

For the last seven years, I have predominantly been a traveler. After a decade of living the big city life in New York and San Francisco, I quit my stressful corporate job, broke up with my tiny studio apartment, and set off to explore the world.

On the surface I was looking for fun, photogenic places to have adventures. But underneath I was running away from loneliness, unhappiness, and the nagging sense that my life had very little meaning or purpose.

I hoped that travel would fill the void, the way it did in books and movies. That it would lead me to love and to a higher calling. (Spoiler alert: It eventually did. But the path in between was disorienting, to put it mildly and without cursing.)

As a single gal with steadily earned savings and a sudden influx of free time, I used those unstructured years of world wandering to "work on myself." It's a fancy way of saying something simple: I wanted more happiness in my life.

So I tried sweaty yoga classes in Bali and silent meditation retreats in Guatemala. I read spiritual texts by Eckhart Tolle, Ram Dass and Yogananda. I trained in the Japanese healing art of Reiki. I even completed an intensive 200-hour yoga teacher training in Costa Rica, becoming the occupational cliché satirized by a report in *The Onion*: "All but 32 women in New York and San Francisco are now certified yoga instructors."

World traveling wasn't all work, of course. I found plenty of time to take surfing lessons in Sri Lanka and Indonesia. I became a PADI Advanced Open Water Diver to explore shipwrecks in the Caribbean and deep-dive with sharks in the Philippines. I learned to play the ukulele, mainly to serenade the stray cats in Morocco and the wild goats in Greece.

I started writing a travel book about these adventures and the lessons learned along the way. It would be a modern mash-up of Elizabeth Gilbert's *Eat, Pray, Love* and Rolf Potts' *Vagabonding: An Uncommon Guide to the Art of Long-Term World Travel.* But midway through the writing process, the pandemic intervened. I stopped traveling and went back to Texas to be with family. It was a strange, surreal time that I will never regret. Particularly the time spent with my grandmother, our daily chats and ukulele duets to John Denver's "Take Me Home, Country Roads"—her unwavering favorite. She died suddenly a few months later while I was on the road again, far from home.

The world had changed, and so had I. When I resumed the nomad life in Mexico, I preferred to travel so slowly that I now behaved more like an expat than a backpacker. My partying days were behind me. I longed to finally find a place, and more than anything, a person, that felt like home. As it turns out, I would find both at the same time.

For years I had been telling friends that I intended to settle on an island somewhere. That all of this traveling was simply location scouting for the right beach town. Then shortly after arriving in Mexico, I began dating a fellow traveler in the same week he decided to stop traveling and buy a hostel. A hostel named La Isla, literally "The Island" in Spanish.

Manifesting has a funny way of giving you exactly what you needed, though not exactly what you asked for. La Isla was nowhere near the ocean. The hostel happened to sit 7,200 feet above sea level, in a historic "Pueblo Magico" in the scenic highlands of Chiapas. After a mere month of dating, we moved into our landlocked island and ran the hostel together for nearly two years, a unique residential experience I describe in Chapter 3.

It's a life I never would have envisioned for myself. Being a hostel mom to hundreds of backpackers and two cats. Managing our volunteer program. Teaching yoga classes to guests. Career-wise, I had pivoted from preparing marketing strategies for some of the world's largest companies to preparing ceremonial cacao drinks for world travelers (Chapters 3 and 9 will explain cacao). My salary took a nosedive, but the health benefits soared.

Amidst the whirlwind of hostel life, I fell in love, made dozens of dear friends, became a decent yoga teacher, and somehow found enough time and clarity to write much of this book.

I feel immense gratitude for finding my "island" home after years of wandering, and immense fortune for finding my partner, Herb, after a decade of singlehood. He has doubled the size of my beaten-down heart and repeatedly stretched my curious mind. As a meditation teacher for over twenty years and a clinical hypnotherapist, Herb has helped me access higher states of consciousness and heal traumas I didn't even know I had (see Chapters 17, 21, 23). I write about the first two years of our relationship in this book, and we are presently cowriting a new life chapter together in Guatemala. It is short a hostel but long on cats (four total), photogenic volcanoes (three right outside our house, gracing the front cover of this book), and the constant sound of construction, as we rush to complete the building of a new lakefront spiritual center.

On Lostness & Foundness

There's a reassuring mantra that originated from Tolkien's *Lord of the Rings* and journeyed afar into travelers' Instagram feeds: *Not all who wander are lost*.

The phrase hints at freedom and adventure, that irresistible upside of travel. Yet during my years of wandering, I came to despise it. The words seemed to taunt me. Not all who wander are lost, *but you are*. I felt lost to ever finding love, life purpose, and a deeper meaning for my existence. My travels were not born out of the lure toward adventure but out of the desire to run away from lostness and loneliness.

My cover story was, in fact, adventure, while secretly I feared that travel was a consolation prize for the life I wanted but had not found. I hinted at this pain to close friends, joking that if I couldn't use my ovaries, I sure as hell was going to use my passport.

Somewhere between the first and second dozen passport stamps, I realized that wandering wasn't a consolation prize at all. It was always meant to be my path. I had to feel lost and lonely *enough* in New York to actually *move*. To try something wildly different. To quote another travelers' mantra, the universe was essentially evicting me from the rut my life had become: *I had to make you uncomfortable or you never would have moved.*

What did I learn throughout my travels—aside that going solo is far less frightening than it sounds (Chapter 13)? I learned that feeling lost is not some unfortunate detour from the path to finding deeper love, happiness, and meaning in your life. Feeling lost is the literal freaking way to find these things. They may be pitted as antonyms in the dictionary, but Lost and Found are not polar opposite states. They are two sides of the same coin. Without darkness there is no light. Without winter there is no spring. We must experience some pain in order to fully understand joy. And without feeling lost, there would be nothing to find.

If you currently feel lost about something, perhaps wondering if you will ever find your romantic partner, find a fulfilling career, or find more lasting happiness within—Congratulations! Feeling lost is the first step to finding anything. Accelerating the other steps in between is why I wrote this book.

Feeling lost nudges us toward our best selves and away from the people and places that no longer serve us. Admitting "I have no idea what I'm doing" may sound like you are back at square one, when in fact you are infinitely farther along than the person who is ignoring their pain or denying their lostness. The person who is attempting to drown it out with work, wine, exercise, movies, shopping, and yes, even travel. I was that person for many years.

ALLA POLSKY

Lost and Found are not opposites, nor are they linear. When I finally found true love, I still felt utterly lost about my life purpose. Sometimes in the span of one hour, or one meditation practice, I go from feeling like giving up to being blissfully present and back again. On more than one occasion, I have ugly-cried uncontrollably and laughed until my abs hurt—at the very same time (see Chapter 17). Your personal growth doesn't have to make sense, and it doesn't always look or feel like progress in the moment.

I named this book *Lost & Found* because I still connect deeply to both states of being. We are constantly learning and evolving—a work in progress—and yet we are, paradoxically, completely perfect exactly where we are.

The work-in-progress part of me swore that I would never write a memoir. Being the opposite of famous, and having nothing truly remarkable and/or traumatizing happen to me (i.e. alien abduction), I feared it would be vaguely self-indulgent and borderline boring to broadcast the details of my life to strangers.

The fear persists, so I have only peppered in personal anecdotes where they seem like teachable moments others could benefit from. I draw as much from personal experience as from the wisdom of my spiritual teachers, favorite authors, and smart friends. This book is part memoir, part other people's alien abductions, and fully a compass for finding more of life's greatest treasures. More love, happiness, meaning.

I have a terrible sense of direction, ask anyone who has traveled with me. But when it comes to my sense of direction in life, I know this much: It was only when I embraced the

LOST & FOUND

lostness, the *I have no idea what I'm doing*, and began loving the parts of me that felt unloved and directionless, that I finally started to find what I was looking for.

On Themes & Contents

This book is separated into five seemingly distinct parts, five major goodies we humans yearn to feel or find: Love, Purpose, Courage, Happiness, and Enlightenment. Of course each area is vast, complex, and entangled with the others. I merely aim to offer a snack-size portion of each weighty topic. A sprinkling of surprising information to feed your higher self.

Reading a billion pages on happiness doesn't make you happy (I tried). Going on a hundred dates doesn't guarantee that you find love (I tried that, too). This book is a pocket guide to maximizing life's magic while minimizing its misery.

Travel will always be one of my passions. Yet in the very act of writing about my travels, they collapsed into one part of a much larger whole. One bumpy, scenic road on the cosmic pursuit of love, purpose, courage, happiness, and enlightenment. It is my greatest wish that the stories and pearls of wisdom in this book help accelerate your own attainment of these treasures. May you find everything you seek, and perhaps something you weren't even looking for.

Alla Polsky
San Marcos La Laguna, Guatemala
July 2023

PART I: FINDING LOVE

This is not a how-to guide on finding love. The last thing anyone needs is more dating tips. The stories in this section are simply ones that changed my views on what it means to love—others and myself—and how it felt when I finally did.

1
I Was Single For A Whole Darn Decade

*Ten years without love taught me a lot.
Here are the highlights.*

When I was 28, I gave a diamond ring back to a guy I loved very much. More than I had ever loved anyone romantically up until that point in my life, and more than I would love anyone again for another ten years.

We shared a great life together in San Francisco. We met at work, got to know each other as friends, and pretty soon could not deny a deeper attraction. The sparks flew on every level: physical, emotional, intellectual. It made me realize how unhealthy and unsatisfying my previous relationships had been. He was my first truly serious partner, and after a few whirlwind months together, I had a strong feeling that he would be my partner for this lifetime.

We moved in together around the one-year mark. Not simply moved in, but bought a two-bedroom apartment together and co-signed on the mortgage. We were *that* sure. Also, housing prices in San Francisco are outrageous for normal non-tech-billionaires to afford on a single income.

LOST & FOUND

On the surface, we were a model couple. We rarely fought, we were affectionate, we cooked dinners together. We didn't seem to tire of each other's company. A blessing, since we worked together, lived together, and had most of the same friends. But beneath the breezy double dates and boozy Napa wine trips, there was always something missing.

We wanted it to work so badly that we continually swept our issues under the rug. Rather than address the growing rift in intimacy, we tried to bridge it with forward motion. See a speed bump? Step on the gas.

At the first sign of relationship trouble, we had bought a home. Playing house and feeling financially committed to each other helped for awhile. At the next sign of trouble a year later, rather than address the deepening rift, we got engaged. I was genuinely shocked when he proposed—we had not been in a good place. But when the man you love wakes you up by slipping a diamond on your finger, you say yes, don't you? I felt optimistic that this romantic milestone would be more than a sparkly Band-aid for our dimming relationship.

There was also talk of getting a puppy, but thankfully the wedding planning was enough to call our bluff. We finally started to talk about the hard stuff. We aired out the intimacy issues and compatibility fears we had been afraid to say out loud for years. As if naming the emotional storm would strengthen it.

Strengthen it did, from partly cloudy skies to a full-blown Category 5 argument in the span of one brutally honest evening. Once we exposed the cracks in our relationship foundation, the entire house of cards came crashing down. We tried couples counseling, but it was too late. We loved each other, that was undeniable. But we were also standing in the way of each other's growth.

Sometimes truly loving someone means letting them go. Even if the timing sucks and a ring has to be returned. The rock itself wasn't actually hard to let go, but fully accepting what it meant would take me years. Accepting that we had reached the end of our soul contract together in this lifetime. Accepting that I could be so wrong about someone I had felt so sure about. Accepting that his highest potential could only be achieved without me, and vice versa. I wasn't ready to accept all of that at once, but I did let him go.

He went off to graduate school and I moved to New York City. I left my heart in San Francisco, as the song goes, but I threw myself heels-first into the prolific dating scene New York is famous for. I longed to get over my ex-fiancé as quickly as possible, hoping to find a new partner to fill the hole in my heart.

But no one did. There were dozens of first dates, a few office flings, and some casual, undefined things that spanned several months. Feelings would fizzle or abruptly change, sometimes on my end, other times on his.

Feeling dejected, I periodically gave up on dating and spent long stretches single and celibate. My job monopolized most of my time and energy, anyway. I was taking time to focus on my career, I reasoned with myself and any nosy relatives concerned about my personal life. I didn't believe it any more than they did.

LOST & FOUND

Seven years after my broken engagement, I wrote an article for the *Huffington Post* called "Why I've Been Single For Seven Years." I hoped that sharing my experience would help others feel less alone. I didn't realize it at the time, but most of what I wrote in that piece was fiction. I was lying to myself along with my readers. I had blamed my single status on external factors. Superficial dating apps. Lopsided gender ratios. Aging past the youthful twenties men prefer. In reality I was still completely closed off. My heart had been shattered in San Francisco, along with my self-worth and my confidence in my own instincts about who was actually right for me.

At the conscious level I wanted to find love again, but at the subconscious level I never wanted to feel that intensity of pain ever again. My heart had decided it would rather be alone than risk getting close to someone. Sadly, my head didn't get the message and continued to date fruitlessly. I was "putting myself out there" logistically but not emotionally.

While traveling in Guatemala around season 8 of Eternally Single, a spiritual teacher told me, "It's actually quite simple. You already have the life you want. If you don't have something you think you want, it's because on some level you don't want it. Sure, a part of you wants to find love, but a bigger part of you does not."

That triggered the crap out of me at the time. At the mental level I was so ready for a partner. So ready not to sleep alone every night, not to travel alone, not to be alone. Yet as Napoleon Hill pointed out in *Think and Grow Rich*, "There is a difference between *wishing* for a thing and being *ready* to receive it." I thought I was ready, but I was merely wishing.

Energetically and vibrationally, I was still walking around with barbed wire around my heart. I pushed promising partners away unconsciously. Instead, and unsurprisingly in retrospect, I mainly attracted men who were emotionally unavailable (sigh), literally unavailable (married—no, thank you), or so overly eager to commit that it was guaranteed to scare me off (in my experience, *Getting Serious* was a horror film, not a romantic comedy).

The same spiritual teacher who told me that I must not actually want a partner also prophesied that my true partner will not appear until I step into my own power and learn to love myself. Otherwise, he warned, we would get sucked into my insecurity dramas. I would lose myself trying to be who I thought he wanted, and it would blow us right out of the water. But we didn't come here to fail, to not be together, my teacher said. So we have an agreement to *wait*.

That four-letter word cut like a slow knife into my hopeful heart. How much longer could I possibly wait than EIGHT YEARS? I asked my teacher without concealing my sadness. I was at my breaking point.

But rather than being broken by it, something shifted. I slowly surrendered to the fact that I had no control over timing. It could take another eight years, or eighty. And it would have nothing to do with my worthiness. All I could do was give myself the love I craved from a partner, whether he ever materialized or not.

Self-love took the form of patience, self-respect, and adventure. The latter came easily with a recently renewed passport full of blank pages. I left Guatemala for Honduras, learned to scuba dive, and followed this new passion to the Philippines, Indonesia and Sri Lanka. I also got very comfortable driving a scooter and sort of comfortable riding a surfboard. Some of my travel writing was published in reputable magazines. I started to feel like the fearless, independent woman I always wished I could be. (To finance this independent lifestyle without draining my savings account, I worked freelance marketing jobs online.)

It's a singular dating strategy articulated in many different ways: don't look for the right person, *become* the right person. Become the person you would want to be with, genuinely loving yourself and your own company. Others will be drawn to that energy. I didn't strategically scheme to become more adventurous just so I could attract the right partner. The diving, surfing, scootering—that was all for me.

Solo travel was invigorating, but with nothing left to prove to myself, I began to travel more and more with an Australian friend I had met in Guatemala. T (short for Tanaya) and I had clicked instantly, dubbing each other as "travel wifey." It felt like a friendship bound by a deeper soul contract, not simply by shared interests.

We explored Morocco, Greece, and Portugal together. We met up in Bali and the Philippines. These places may sound like paradise, but we both went through tough times emotionally. Family health scares, work stress, romantic droughts and doubts. Our bond made it all bearable. I have always felt lucky in friendship, if not in love.

I also began to find comfort and renewed patience in a dawning realization: even if I was fully ready to meet my guy—truly loving myself and honoring the woman I was becoming—perhaps *he* was not ready *for me* yet. Perhaps he, or both of us, still had some underlying issues to heal on our own. Some last layers of inner work to resolve independently before we met.

Ironically, we *had* already met. Back in Guatemala. I just wouldn't know he was meant to be my partner for another two years. Here are the lengths the universe will go to keep you and your true partner apart until you are both ready:

The day Herb and I met, I felt a connection. We were paired together to practice some energy techniques at a mutual friend's informal cacao ceremony (yes, this is what modern hippies do for fun—Chapters 3 and 9 will explain cacao in more detail). I hoped this tall, man-bunned Spiritual Guy wasn't intuitive enough to read minds, because mine was smitten.

After the group gathering, we walked to a nearby café and continued getting to know each other. The conversation flowed as freely as the kombucha—but Herb seemed to suddenly lose interest after my Australian travel wife arrived. Soon after I introduced her, he excused himself. He began talking to another young woman and didn't return.

I felt snubbed and slightly rejected but didn't dwell on it for long. We had only just met that day, after all. My hopeful radar on meeting my match had already been wrong for nearly a decade, after all. What harm was one more miss?

Fast forward two years later. The pandemic is in full swing. Herb is sheltering in place in a Colombian jungle, and I on a Floridian beach. We have not spoken to each other since that day we met in Guatemala at a cacao ceremony. In a pandemic world, the ceremonies have gone virtual, and we see each other through a video screen after two years apart. I share a recent dating debacle with the group and an overarching doubt about my judgment with men. Herb messages me during the ceremony, thanking me for my candor and reviving the banter we had started at that lakefront café years ago.

"Can I ask you a personal question?" he writes in our chat box the next day.

"Of course," I reply, eager to get more personal. I have no clue what he could possibly want to know.

It is less a question and more a confession. "When we met in Guatemala, I thought you were into women. You introduced that Australian girl as your wife."

Oh my god, I say out loud. I may have typed it to him as well.

"I said TRAVEL wife! It's a nickname!"

I quickly clarify that I have always been into MEN, not women. We exchange a string of laughing emojis. I wonder if tears are more appropriate. Because in that moment I realize that what I had interpreted as him rejecting me on the day we met, was merely him stepping aside when my "wife" showed up. He walked away because of three giant misconceptions: *This cute girl I kinda like only likes women, is currently married to a woman, and it appears I have no chance here.*

With my sexual orientation cleared up, our online banter takes an unmistakably flirty turn. We start talking on the phone. We talk for hours almost every day for several months. We both steer our travel plans toward Mexico, arriving within a day of each other, albeit in separate parts of the country. Eventually we converge in the same town. From the first week we spend together, it's clear that this is going to be something. We are both ready for this. But for a long time we weren't.

We still joke about the two years we spent apart because of a teensy miscommunication.

"Remember back when you were a lesbian?" he teases.

"Don't you pride yourself on being Mister Intuitive Mind Reader?" I fire back. "How did you misread such a big thing?"

He didn't, though. I believe the universe was making us wait by any means necessary. We had both needed that extra time. He needed to get back together with an ex and fully close that romantic chapter. I needed to travel solo and fully surrender to loving myself without the guarantee of anyone else ever loving me as well.

If a seer with psychic powers had told me right after my broken engagement that I would be single for another ten years, I would have said, "Please throw your heavy crystal ball directly at my skull and put me out of my misery." But if she had also shown me the partner in my distant future and how it would feel to be together, I may have mustered up the will to wait.

There is no crystal ball, of course. I have no idea if we will be together for fifty years like we sweetly envision during pillow talk. But I know the underlying energy of this relationship is unlike anything I have felt before. It is irresistibly magnetic and nakedly honest and surprisingly easy, even when it's hard.

After I shared the amusing slow-start tale of how Herb and I met with some of our hostel volunteers, one of them asked me an interesting question: "Was there a moment you knew that your heart was finally opening after all those years, finally ready for this special relationship?"

I had never thought about it before, but the answer came to me instantly. I told her I knew it when my heart was still scared shitless but no longer wanted to *hide*. I knew I would not, and could not, hide from this man. I was ready to show him the real me. If we got together, there would be no games, no shields, no filters. And if this real me, insecurities and baggage in tow, did not scare him off, then I would know that he was the person I had been waiting all this time for.

There is one part of the *Huffington Post* piece I wrote that was fully the truth, as true then as it is now. I had ended the article with this:

On some level, I know I needed to be single for an absurdly long time to learn hard lessons about life that could not be learned any other way. So what I'm left with is faith in the universe and its timing, even if it, like me, can be unfashionably late.

Lessons after ten absurdly long years of being single:

ALLA POLSKY

1. Sometimes loving someone means letting them go. If they are the ones letting you go, and you wish they would stay, trust that their departure is a gift, not a punishment. You both are meant for more fulfilling partnerships. I'm not saying to give up on something with potential or to stop working on your relationship. Only you know deep down when something is beyond repair or time to be set free. Your emotional courage will be rewarded with something far greater than you can presently imagine.

2. You might think you are ready for that next relationship. You might even feel ready. But if you're not in it yet, energetically you are not ready yet. Or your future partner is not ready, still working on themselves to be ready for you. Respect the process and honor that timeline for both of you. It will be worth it. (Please note, I am not saying there is anything *wrong* with you if you are single for a long time. Nor is it your *fault*. But something in your energy may be out of alignment which is pushing people away unconsciously. Mine certainly was. Making it conscious is a vital step toward resolving it.)

3. Don't give up hope, but do give up the struggle. Don't force yourself on dates you don't want, nor force a relationship with someone you don't love because you don't want to be alone. If someone rejects you, they are not meant for you. In the words of Rumi, *What you seek is seeking you.* In the words of your five-year-old self, *Row, row, row your boat, gently down the stream*. Surrendering to the natural pace and

direction of your life's romantic current, rather than fighting against it, will save you a lot of needless flailing and suffering.

4. It sounded too cheesy to be true until it happened to me: If two people have an agreement to meet in this lifetime, a soul contract to fulfill, there is not a darn thing you can do to miss that meeting or mess it up by saying or doing the wrong thing. (Accidentally delaying it with a little misunderstanding about a wife? That's another thing.) You WILL meet, and you will get as many chances as it takes to break old patterns, learn from each other, and fully step into your own power.

5. When it's the right person, your heart will unbreak (and theirs will, too). After decades of rejection, disappointment, and unfulfilling dates, my heart was so tired. I was afraid I had no energy or desire left to fall in love again. I prayed that my weary heart would muster up the strength for the right person. When he finally came along, loving him wasn't even a choice. It was as easy as breathing. As we help each other shed any lingering layers of heart-fatigue, that ease continues to deepen.

6. You know you have found a true soulmate when they are not scared or turned off by your real, unfiltered self. On the contrary, they love you even more for being brave and vulnerable enough to show your true self. The one with flaws, insecurities, and traumas. Of course it goes both ways. You also love your partner more, not less, as they reveal their whole self to you (assuming there is no abuse).

7. With the right person, there's no tip-toeing around certain issues, and no need to follow silly dating codes. Herb and I moved in together after one month of dating—into the tiniest private room in our hostel. It wasn't always easy, but we learned to regularly air out our emotional triggers and clear up issues immediately, before they could fester and grow. Relationships are practically designed to bring your unprocessed emotional issues and insecurities to the surface. If both partners are willing to take responsibility for their own while helping each other feel supported and understood, then the relationship thrives.

8. Lastly, it sounds trite but it's annoyingly true: love yourself like you want to be loved. Don't hold back that love until you become the person you want to be. Love yourself for who you already are, and the personal growth you desire will come more easily than by withholding that love until you reach those desired changes. *Self-love is meant to be our default setting, not a conditional reward for good behavior.* I had to love myself enough to actually allow myself to have a partner as amazing as Herb. When someone amazing comes into your life, can you allow them in instead of pushing their love away because deep down you don't believe you deserve it?

If you are currently single, I would bet serious money on the odds of you finding your partner in well under a decade. And if you are wondering if you met them already, trust in the cosmic timing of things unfolding when you're both ready.

LOST & FOUND

The universe has a sense of humor. It may tease you a little—it teases me a lot—but it is always on your side. The side of love.

2

SYNCHRONICITY DOES NOT MEAN IT'S FATE

Sometimes you were meant to meet, but not meant to be

Toward the end of my single decade, a good friend set me up with a guy. She knew me really well, and knew him well enough to think we might hit it off.

As I got to know him, the crazy coincidences kept stacking up. Manhattan has 214 numbered streets. We had lived on the *same exact one* for years. We took classes at the same yoga studio. Knew many of the same people.

We had circled around each other but never met. Until now. There were oddly specific parallels in our childhoods and family backgrounds, too. But the clincher for me was this: in college I foolishly got a tattoo of a certain fruit, more or less on a dare. The guy's last name literally translates to this fruit in German, where his ancestry originated.

Too random to be just chance, right? Mister and Mrs. Fruit. It felt meant-to-be-ish. We had both spent years being single and discerning, yearning for something deeper. Suddenly we found ourselves exchanging cheesy texts containing words like *soulmate*.

A wink from the universe

The term synchronicity was coined by analytical psychologist Carl Jung. He introduced the concept during a 1930 lecture and made it a focal point of his work in the early 1950s.

Jung used synchronicity to describe circumstances that "appear meaningfully related yet lack a causal connection."[1] In essence, something happens that feels like it's too meaningful to merely be a coincidence. It seems to defy the laws of probability. *Never tell me the odds of THAT*, you think.

We all experience this on occasion. Random run-ins. Eerily timed coincidences. One-in-a-million chance encounters. A few years back my sister ran into one of my close friends on the street. In Rome. Both were passing through on holiday.

While living in New York I once missed a subway train by a nanosecond. Like any New Yorker, I waited impatiently for the next train in three minutes. The subway car I chose was packed, but I instantly recognized an old colleague I had not seen in years. We caught up, and I got a job offer from the encounter.

In his youth Herb once went hunting with his dad and left his binoculars at home. They were miles from any trails where other humans normally go when he lamented out loud, "Man, I wish I had some binoculars." In that exact moment, a pair peeked out in the snow. Someone had dropped theirs in the same spot, presumably while running from a Yeti. (Herb would like my readers to know that he no longer hunts. I would like my readers to know that Herb is nearly the same height as a Yeti.)

These harmless synchronicities tend to brighten up our day and make for good stories at dinner parties. But when they involve romance, it's not always so harmless.

The stars don't always align forever
My friend John recently went through a painful breakup. He told me the way they met was crazy. "All the stars just aligned. We had all of these people and places in common. It felt like the universe was pushing us together. It has to mean something, right?" Deep down he admits the relationship was unhealthy, but he still can't quite believe it didn't work out.

Synchronicity means you were meant to meet, not necessarily meant to be.

I believe the circumstances that bring two people together are designed to be attention-grabbing enough that you don't miss the meeting. But there's no clause in the synchronicity contract that says it's supposed to be Forever.

We can partly blame our entertainment culture for the misconception. Fairy tales where love conquers impossible odds. Romantic comedies with ridiculous meet-cute scenarios and titles like *Serendipity*. We never see what happens after the movie ends, but many of us have been disappointed by the absence of the Happily part in our own Ever Afters.

That guy my friend set me up with, Mr. Synchronicity with the fruity last name? I wasn't afraid to put myself out there. After a month of increasingly intimate phone calls and video dates, I flew to Florida to meet him in person. We were both hopeful that there could be a real connection beyond the wild coincidences that initially bonded us.

We crashed and burned. It didn't take long to realize we were completely wrong for each other. Annoyingly, he knew it before I did.

He wasn't meant to be my partner. He was meant to get me out to Florida. In an optimistic splurge, I had pre-paid for a monthlong apartment rental near the ocean. I envisioned long, romantic walks on the beach. But we called it quits about one week in. I found myself with lots of alone time, feeling a bit rejected but mainly looking for answers. *Why was my relationship radar so off?* I joined a virtual gathering led by a spiritual teacher I had met while living in Guatemala several years back. He had been a source of wisdom and guidance before, so I hoped that sharing my latest letdown would provide further clarity and comfort. Talking about my personal life in front of forty strangers brings me about as much joy as getting a publicly televised root canal. But desperate for answers, I spoke up.

Of course they weren't all strangers. I don't remember my teacher's exact guidance, but I do remember exactly what happened a few minutes later. A guy named Herb, who looked even more ruggedly handsome than I remembered, sent me a private message to thank me for the courage to share my story with the group. We had not spoken to each other in two years, and if you read the previous chapter, you know why we had stopped talking in the first place. The next day, we began talking nonstop.

ALLA POLSKY

If I didn't have a recent dating flop that compelled me to speak up during the group gathering, my dream guy would have continued to believe I had no interest in men.

Fast forward another two years, and you already know we are going strong. It's the most honest and fulfilling relationship I have ever had. We didn't first meet in a sparks-flying-synchronicity (the sparks being deflected by my travel wife), but we sure reconnected with fireworks. As we caught up on the details of how our paths had diverged since the initial meeting, it became clear we had both needed those years apart. To be alone, to be with others, to grow and heal, and ultimately to be ready for this special relationship.

Sometimes you are meant to meet a seemingly special someone in order to help you recognize an unhealthy pattern in your life and progress to your own next level of awesomeness. Other times you might encounter patterns not in people but in numbers, symbols, words, or images.

In Jung's view of analytical psychology, "the recognition of seemingly meaningful coincidences is a mechanism by which unconscious material is brought to the attention of the conscious mind."[2] In other words, synchronicity has a purpose. The universe is trying to get your attention. It can't always reach you directly, so it enlists the help of patterns that will feel meaningful to some part of your being. The same set of numbers might tease your awareness throughout the day, like 11 and 22 do for me. They pop up comically often as flight numbers, seat numbers, and the time on my phone (it's always 11:22). When I feel particularly lost or need extra reassurance, I meet people with these numbers literally tattooed on their body.

Earlier today I struggled with editing this chapter. I was looking for any reason to quit. I pushed my book aside and watched *Hustle*, the new Adam Sandler movie. What was his character's nickname and basketball jersey, the numerical glue of the entire film? 22. Then I realized that today's date happened to be 6/11/22. Well played, Universe. I will keep writing as long as Adam Sandler keeps making fantastic movies again.

For you it might not be a number. Maybe it's a recurring symbol, an animal, a particular word, a certain smell. Whatever it is, you can't help but notice it. And your conscious mind can't help but wonder, "Am I crazy or does that mean something?"

You're not crazy. Synchronicity is often a sign that you are on the right track, whatever that track means for you. Keep going. If the sign happens to involve crossing paths with a certain person on the other side of the world, or meeting someone who appears to share unbelievable parallels with your own life, there *is* a reason you were meant to meet on this exact path right now. However, it is *not* an assurance that this person will be in your life forever, nor that this path will be free of speed bumps, roadblocks, and gaping potholes. On the contrary, often you must go through the bumpy road to get to amazing outcomes and experiences in your future.

ALLA POLSKY

The bottom line

Synchronicity is both magical and misunderstood. It's a nudge in the right direction, not an assurance that you have reached the finish line. Those strange little signs and coincidences are crucial stepping stones guiding you up to something marvelous at the summit. I had to step on a lot of stones to get to Herb (and not just because he is a giant).

Was the journey slower and more painful than I would have wanted? Hell yes. His was, too. But it's the journey we both needed, following our own little synchronicities until we were ready for the big, interconnected one. We learned lessons along the way that would make our relationship infinitely easier and stronger. (For example, Mister Fruit taught me never to take rejection personally. On some level, he was just getting out of the way because Herb was getting ready to swoop in.)

As you begin tuning in more deeply to the natural forces guiding you, being more fully present and trusting the timing of your life, amusing synchronicities will illuminate your path. I won't be getting any more fruit tattoos, but perhaps something island-themed is in order, as you will see in the next chapter.

3

MANIFESTING DOESN'T NEED DETAILS

How I got exactly what I needed, but not what I asked for

As I mentioned in the introduction, manifesting is a clever mistress. For years I had dreamed of falling in love and settling together on an island somewhere. Perhaps opening a dive shop or a beachfront bed-and-breakfast.

Well, the island part definitely got lost in translation, and I don't mean from English to Spanish. In the same week that Herb and I met up in Mexico and officially started dating, he felt cosmically guided to buy a local hostel named La Isla (literally "The Island" in Spanish). Our island hostel happened to be high up in the mountains, nowhere near an ocean. But it became exactly the home we needed for our relationship, individual growth, and future business partnership.

Here is a little glimpse into a typical day in the life I could never have seen coming, nor thought to pin onto a vision board.

When your home is also a hostel

ALLA POLSKY

Our alarm goes off at 6:30 AM. The sun has just peeked over the mountains. We dress comfy-warm, grab some blankets and yoga mats, and head to the outdoor terrace for group morning practice. Silent sun salutations followed by seated meditation with the hostel's longer term residents.

I play a daily game of Whack-a-Mole with my chatty mind, trying to vanquish thoughts the moment they arise. I succeed sporadically. But mostly I fail and spend 30 minutes thinking instead of meditating. *I will meditate better tomorrow*, I think to myself. *Whack!*

Then it's breakfast time. Banana oat pancakes with local honey. Chia pudding with fruit. The fragrant coffee Chiapas is famous for. After over a year of living at the hostel, I still marvel at the delicious perks we include with each nightly stay—about $7 US for a dorm bed. Herb and I usually leave the free food for guests and volunteers, but we love to get coffee and socialize.

At the shared dining table, I meet a young couple from France. A guy from Argentina. Several long-term travelers who can't quite pinpoint where "home" is anymore. What's everyone up to today? Local markets and easy hikes. Spanish classes. A boat trip through a nearby canyon.

There is small talk interspersed with big talk. Life plans redirected by the pandemic. Uncertain futures. Upset stomachs adjusting to the crappy water in town. "I even brushed my teeth with the tap water in *India*," I say, "but here you reeeally can't. Even the locals get drinking water delivered like our hostel."

LOST & FOUND

Four mornings a week, our guests enjoy a complimentary yoga class on the sunny terrace. Two mornings a week, we hold cacao ceremonies. Today is such a morning. "What exactly IS a cacao ceremony?" someone asks. I start to explain, then stop myself. "It's better to experience it with your own eyes and taste buds," I tease, while chopping up a solid block of 100% pure cacao. The scent of serious chocolate fills the hostel.

I measure out each ceremonial serving on a tiny scale—precisely 42.5 grams (1.5 ounces)—and pour the powder into handcrafted clay mugs. The cacao will melt perfectly with a bit of hot water and await seasoning if desired. We offer honey, cinnamon, panela sugar, and spicy chili powder.

The ceremony is on the hostel's outdoor terrace. A sea of floor pillows and blankets quickly fills with forty curious souls. About half are cacao virgins. The others have been here before, or been to other spiritual events that incorporate cacao, like ecstatic dances and music kirtans.

"The journey today is about going inward, not outward," Herb tells the group. He leads each ceremony with a special blend of meditation, storytelling, and shamanic journeying. He would never call himself a shaman or a healer, though people less biased than his girlfriend commonly contend that he has extraordinary gifts.

Cacao is considered a psychoactive plant medicine, infinitely more gentle than the psychedelic varieties (ayahuasca, peyote, mushrooms). Cacao will not push you into your healing process until you are truly ready to go there. Today many of our attendees are ready. There is crying, laughing, screaming, shaking. People releasing pain and traumas they are largely unaware of at the conscious level. People receiving knowings, upgrades, and guidance from within. The event must look and sound crazy to bystanders (and even to some of us experiencing it firsthand.)

No one wants to leave when the ceremony is over. *What the heck did you do to us?* I ask Herb. It's a running joke now. I know he can't explain it in words. And even if he could, this experience is not for the rational mind to 'figure out.' It's for a deeper level of our consciousness. A state beyond that of thoughts and even beyond feelings.

Most days it feels like Herb and I adopted two cats and twenty-five backpackers overnight. Except our children's faces keep changing and many speak languages we can't understand. Some stay for a few days, but many end up extending for a few weeks or even months.

On some level I feel responsible for their happiness and well-being while they're here. Not so they will leave good reviews online, but because they are guests in my home. Even though none of them actually know it's my home when they first arrive.

"So, do you like, *work here?*" I am asked with amusing regularity.

For some reason I fumble the answer every time. I pause a little too long. "Sort of?" I reply. "I live here, I work here, I play here." I'm not sure there's a nice, neat label for the gal who paints the events posters, prepares cacao, teaches yoga, and happens to live with the hostel's owner on the top floor.

I have been nicknamed The Hostel Fairy. The Hostel Princess. Hostel Mom. I have suggested First Lady of the Hostel, but it has yet to catch on.

Our foster kids range in ages from 18 to 80. Skewing younger, naturally. But ours is not a party hostel, and it attracts all kinds of fascinating people from every corner of the globe. Some have been traveling for years. Others have just begun.

Many have been re-routed far from where they were headed pre-pandemic, both geographically and spiritually. Most are looking for something deeper, whether consciously aware of it or not. They all chose a hostel with free yoga and meditation classes, with images of Ganesh and Gandhi in the living room.

I like to describe our hostel as not simply a place to sleep, but a place to awaken. Awaken to deeper states of consciousness. To living more fully in the present. To the oneness that connects us all.

I had avoided this hippie-dippy-sounding spiritual stuff for years, working the corporate grind in big cities for a decade, then burning out and traveling solo around the world. Now I'm not only buying into the whole spiritual lifestyle, I'm even selling it to others. Annoyingly to my old corporate self, I have never felt happier or less alone.

My home is like a hostel meets ashram meets community center meets TV sitcom about a hostel-ashram-community. Picture the cast of *Friends*, except they all hang out in a hostel instead of a coffee shop. Naturally there are more Phoebes than Rosses. No one seems to have a demanding job, and there's no shortage of random dramas or hilarious hijinks. My days can be summed up by episode names like The One With The Smelly Guy Who Refused To Shower and The One Where The Cat Leaves A Dead Bird On My Yoga Mat.

In a hostel the faces change constantly. People check in and check out. We are fully booked almost every night. The only regularly appearing cast of characters in this strange sitcom are Herb and I, the longtime housekeeper, and the hostel's two cats.

There are six rotating volunteers who stay for free as a work-exchange, helping run the hostel while working on their own personal growth. They are really here for the six-week spiritual residency program Herb and I created, an immersive 'soul school' where people can transform their lives while living at the hostel.

Our spiritual residents learn and practice meditation, yoga, lucid dreaming, shadow work, and goal-setting. They heal traumas, start creative or business projects, access higher states of consciousness, and make lifelong friendships. Some even find love. We have already hosted fifty residents from over twenty-five countries. On the more exhausting days, I remind myself that we are doing something meaningful, something that helps people make lasting changes in their lives.

In a hostel, everything else is fleeting. Things constantly break, like toilets and kitchen appliances. Things mysteriously disappear, like room keys and wine openers. Even people disappear, like the guy who left his luggage and guitar here six months ago. Police were notified.

LOST & FOUND

There are loud guests, messy guests, needy guests, and easy guests. Mainly easy guests. I am sincerely sad to see many of them go.

In a hostel, friendships are measured by openness, not by time. It's amazing how fast people go from complete strangers to dear friends. To dear family, really. I am constantly making friends and losing friends as they travel onward. But when time together is short and transient, walls come down faster. We would rather be ourselves, be vulnerable, than be cool.

In a hostel, everything is shared. Shared dorm rooms and bathrooms. Shared living rooms. A shared kitchen full of communal cookware. A communal guitar that hangs on the wall in the rare moments when it's not being played. By my conservative estimate, about 85% of world travelers are talented musicians.

Shared books. We have a communal library where travelers freely take books and leave books. Shared clothes. There's a wooden crate near the reception desk where people leave clothes they no longer want, and others find new treasures. Shared food. A communal basket and fridge drawer where people leave items they no longer need. Shared meals. A "family dinner" every Sunday to get to know each other.

The only one who doesn't like to share is our hostel cat Greta. For her size she hogs an impressive amount of space on our bed every night—and gets territorial if her brother Leon tries to join the slumber party.

Admittedly, there is not a ton of peaceful slumber for this light sleeper, with a rowdy bar across the street. Herb, a hypnotherapist, actually hypnotized me to get less triggered by the noise. It still wakes me up, but rather than get angry about it, I simply drift back to sleep.

Some days the hostel life feels like a circus. A lively parade of people and pets. But most days, it just feels like home.

The day I met Herb, he described my energy as warm, staticky socks out of the dryer. I frowned, thinking, what girl wants to be likened to *socks*?

He had meant that I remind him of home. And now, years later, that's how it feels to live in this hostel together. Like slipping on warm socks on a cold day. Like home.

·»—·♦·—«·

The life I had dreamed of didn't involve needing warm socks. It was set on a tropical island. The life I had dreamed of didn't involve living in a crowded hostel with backpackers half my age. Now some of those young backpackers have become as dear as family. And after years of traveling in the tropics, the break from the heat and mosquitos has been a treat.

As discussed in the previous chapter, synchronicities don't always spell forever, simply that you are on the right track. The synchronicity of the "island" hostel is now leading us somewhere familiar yet wholly unexpected. Herb and I are relocating to the Guatemalan lakeside town where we first met, San Marcos La Laguna. We have bought a house about five yoga mat lengths away from the exact spot where we first laid eyes on each other five years earlier.

Only time will tell if the hostel's most enduring creation shall be my first draft of this book, my relationship with Herb, or the new business baby we conceived together while running La Isla. We are evolving the spiritual program we created in the hostel. It will be offered as a monthlong live-in course in our new lakefront property. Herb has also created a year-long intensive apprenticeship for those who want to harness the real power of cacao, meditation, and hypnosis as therapeutic modalities. We are calling it The Black Lotus: shadow work for light workers. It will be a place where people come to resolve their own shadows—the mainly unconscious patterns, traumas, and emotional blocks that hold us back from love, happiness, success—and a place where people learn to help others do the same. It's like a Hogwarts for healers, I tell people after they have mis-categorized it as a retreat center.

The Black Lotus is another life curveball I didn't see coming. One that could only be pitched from our homey hostel. La Isla will always be where we fell in love, put down roots, and planted the seed for something special. Unfortunately it became too difficult to split our time and energy between two businesses in two different countries, so we made the tough decision to sell the hostel. It is now in good hands with a new owner who was previously a longtime guest. "I have always dreamed of owning a hostel, I just never thought it would happen right now, here in Mexico," he told us in a daze.

In manifesting your dream life, don't get overly attached to the details in your head or specific images on your vision board. Leave room for the universe to surprise you. To give you exactly what you *need* at this stage of your life, not exactly what you think you want. It might look very different than you envisioned. Not just different, but better.

ALLA POLSKY

After Herb and I had been dating for about a year, I remembered I had once made a list of qualities I desired in my dream partner. After actively avoiding this sort of cheesy, itemized love wish-list for decades, a close friend gifted me a reading with an astrologer who strongly urged me to create one. "How can the universe know what you want if *you* don't?" she asked. So I compiled a list of qualities and soon forgot about it.

Reading my list again after five years, I was shocked:

- Loves travel like I do, open to living abroad
- Someone spiritual but not religious
- Can sense energy or something larger than ourselves
- We have a house and a business together

I had planted the seeds for meeting Herb and running our spiritual business abroad without any idea what physical form those seeds would sprout. I suppose I could have written "We run a yoga studio together or a retreat center or a kombucha brewery." But the details didn't matter. I just knew I wanted to mix business and pleasure with my partner. I had always longed for the kind of relationship where we could build something together rather than driving off to separate offices every day. (This longing may explain my unconscious tendency to date coworkers before I met Herb.)

It is tempting to dream in specifics. Imagining what your partner might look like. What your dream house or job will look like. But what we are really after is the energy behind those things. Not what they will look like, but what *you* will *feel* like. Loved, supported, appreciated, inspired, uplifted. Fully seen and fully home. These types of feelings often await you in a future or a partner that looks nothing like you envisioned—and feels even better than you imagined.

Maybe one day I will find my literal island home. Herb and I are both inexplicably drawn toward sailing around the world, despite currently possessing about forty-five minutes of combined sailing experience. I will leave the details to the wind. Whatever happens, I suspect our life will be neither predictable nor dull.

4

SELF-LOVE DOESN'T MAKE YOU A NARCISSIST

It might sound obvious, but it's a lesson I learned the hard way

Growing up, I remember watching TV with my mom and my aunt, hearing them say things like, "Wow, this woman has a lot of self-confidence for her size and/or looks."

These comments were not intended as insults. I detected genuine surprise and even a hint of jealousy toward these on-screen women exuding authentic pride in their less-than-perfect appearance. (Okay, some of these sassy starlets may have been guests on a daytime talk show about trailer park love triangles or heated paternity disputes, but still. The self-love was *real*.)

The women in my family embodied an all-too-common phenomenon: they tended to focus on what they didn't like about themselves instead of what they did like. So did all of my friends, and all the women on TV, except for those overly confident unicorns on *Jerry Springer*. My already insecure little girl brain translated this to mean, "Self-love is a form of self-delusion if you have any observable flaws." I held on to this unconscious belief well into adulthood, no matter how many compliments or reassurances I received from loved ones about my appearance. They were biased, after all, having played a direct role in passing on the features I was most unsatisfied with.

I had always felt self-conscious about my slightly downturned nose, which resulted in not one, but two rhinoplasty consultations with top plastic surgeons in New York and Dallas. I chickened out both times, but the insecurity lingered. With all the time I wasted wishing for a different nose or trying to reverse the drooping with my finger, I could have probably learned to speak fluent Mandarin or found a promising cure for cancer.

My naturally curly, borderline frizzy, hair was another constant source of insecurity and self-whatever-you-call-the-opposite-of-love. Over the years I spent hundreds of hours flat-ironing it to be straight—and thousands of dollars to have it chemically straightened in salons once my salary could justify the expense.

As we move further down the female body, countless other insecurities and reasons not to love myself appeared. I realize that when we talk about self-love, the emphasis is usually on loving the inside or the whole person, not a superficial love of your outside appearance. But for me the distinction did not exist. I took any observable imperfection on my human meat suit as admissible evidence in the case of Why Alla Would Be Crazy To Love Herself, inside or out.

On the other extreme, to me it felt vaguely narcissistic to be in love with yourself, whether your physical features, personality, or overall being. What little I knew about the Greek tragedy of Narcissus involved this son of gods becoming so enchanted with his own reflection in a pool of water that he forgot to feed himself and DIED. Surely it was safer to love thyself too little than too much?

Meanwhile, I was having no trouble remembering to feed myself. In college I gained the cautionary Freshman Fifteen (pounds). On my petite 5'2" frame it might as well have been the Freshman Fifty. When tactless family friends or relatives commented on my visible weight gain during visits home, it felt like being punched on the sensitive insides I was already looking for reasons not to love.

Unsurprisingly, when it came to dating, I did the one thing you are really not supposed to do: look for love and validation outside of yourself.

If you want to find love, first find it within. Love yourself like you want to be loved. I found these platitudes annoying and almost infuriating. They were blatantly false. I knew plenty of couples in which one or both partners harbored deep insecurities, low self-esteem, and virtually no trace of self-love. My own mother immediately came to mind. She yo-yo dieted, despised having her picture taken, and her opinion of herself on the inside wasn't much rosier. "How did *I* manage to have such smart children?" she would ask without a trace of sarcasm when my sister and I brought home straight-A report cards.

Despite her self-perceived shortcomings, my father has always loved her deeply, genuinely seeing her beauty radiate from inside and out. The rest of us do, too. (To be clear, I am not blaming my struggles with self-love on my mother—she had her own struggles, but she was always my biggest fan. If there is any truth to the notion that you must learn to love yourself before you can fully love another, she must have a secret stockpile of self-love hidden somewhere, because I have always received the deepest, most unconditional, non-judgmental love a daughter could possibly get from a mother.)

While I was busy trying to poke holes in the logic of those self-love clichés, I was missing their entire point. It's not *Love yourself so that it's easier and more appealing for someone else to love you.* It's not *Love yourself just in case no one else will.* There is no "so that" or "in case." Your own love comes with no attached strings, and it's not a consolation prize.

My partner Herb offers another compelling reason to love yourself, should you require additional incentive: **there is a part of you that *only you* can love.** The parts that you find hardest to love, those which you constantly put down or ignore, are the parts that can only be truly healed with your own love. No amount of external validation from partners, family, or followers will be able to fill that void permanently.

What if you can't bring yourself to love those parts of you that you hate? For me it was my nose, my hair, my anxiety and overthinking. Then can you at least love the part of you that is so hard on yourself, the part that doesn't know how to fully love or accept yourself yet?

For years I resisted this woo-woo self-love crap. Instead I fed my insecurities, frequently said mean things to myself in the mirror that rhyme with fugly, and secretly hoped a man would one day prove me wrong. Instead I attracted partners who seemed to prove me right, mirroring my lack of self-love and respect. I used their bad treatment of me to reinforce my own feelings of low self-worth, and the painful cycle continued until I learned the hard way that loving myself is a win-win situation.

If someone rejects you, you love yourself enough not to take it personally. You even start to see it as a favor. They are stepping out of your life to make space for someone who is meant for you. Someone who will love you on a level you didn't know existed. Until that person arrives, you love yourself. After that person arrives, you still love yourself.

Our relationship is mostly smooth sailing now, but when Herb and I first started dating, he was unsure of his feelings for me. I said the big *I love you* about three months in. My mind didn't plan to say it, but my mouth just blurted out the thing my heart already knew with certainty. He told me that he was happy in our relationship, but he did not want to say it back until he was absolutely sure. That sureness didn't arrive until the six-month mark.

The three months in between my *I love you* and his saw some stormy seas. They took the wind out of my sails, if you catch my drift. (Last nautical metaphor, I swear.) Those months tested my faith in our relationship, but never my faith in myself.

During those three months I realized how much I had grown in the self-love department. Yes, I was sad that he was still unsure. Yes, I dearly wanted my love to be reciprocated. But I didn't mistake his uncertainty for evidence that I was *unworthy of love*. That's what the old me would have done.

LOST & FOUND

The new me seemed to know instinctively deep down that his uncertainty had nothing to do with me. It was his own emotional baggage. His own confusion about his feelings. His own fear of being hurt again, or hurting someone else.

I tried my best to honor his process and his timeline. To not need him to change on my terms. I continued to love him, and myself. And my patience paid off like Apple stock in the early 2000s.

Since the day Herb told me he loved me, too, and thanked me for being in his life (and for being so patient with him), our relationship has deepened exponentially. Not in spite of the shaky start, but in part because of it. He saw that I could love him without conditions or strings attached, while I saw, to my own surprise, that I actually loved myself. At least enough to not blame myself for someone else's uncertainty.

When my spiritual teacher in Guatemala had warned me years before that if I didn't learn to love myself, my own insecurities would doom my next relationship, I believe he was referring to this moment.

If things had gone the other way and Herb had never said it back, we might have gone our separate ways. But I would never regret loving him, nor loving myself through the pain of a broken heart.

He did say it back, thank Cupid, and continues to say it daily. He even says words I longed to hear my whole life— beautiful, gorgeous—and he inexplicably adores the parts of me I have hated. The aforementioned hair and nose, for instance. Seeing myself through his loving eyes does not change how I see myself. I still wish I had silky straight hair and probably always will. But I also honor and appreciate myself exactly as I am. And when Herb calls me beautiful, I allow myself to fully believe him without feeling like Narcissus.

Imposter Syndrome: another self-love saboteur

There is a popular Venn diagram floating around the internet with two overlapping circles. One circle contains ABSOLUTE NARCISSISM and the other CRIPPLING SELF-DOUBT. In the overlapping center is the word ART.

It's a powerful insight into the minds of artists, musicians, writers and creators of all kinds. The messy creative process of birthing something entirely new into the world is riddled with highs and lows. Moments of intense clarity when you feel like you are a genius, and moments of paralyzing struggle when you feel like a complete fraud who should probably give up and start all over again (or never again). Sometimes both types of feelings grip you simultaneously, genius and fraud, making you wonder if you are going crazy—not a wholly unwelcome prospect since many legendary artists were certifiably nuts.

If you are unsure whether you are personally afflicted with Imposter Syndrome, also called Inferiority Complex, just try to write a book. Insecurities you didn't even know you had will creep up during the writing process. (*Am I boring? Long-winded? Unoriginal? Wait, do I use too many metaphors or not enough?*)

I want to briefly highlight this inferiority thing because it afflicts far more than just the creative class of writers and artists. It seems virtually everybody has some form of I'm Not Good

Enough or I Don't Belong Here, whether it pertains to their confidence at work, school, hobbies, or in their relationships (or lack thereof).

And sure, there is a healthy level of self-awareness where you acknowledge that there are ways you could improve your job skills, your study habits, or your attentiveness as a loving partner. I personally used to operate far below this healthy level. My acute case of imposter syndrome, mixed in with the insecurities about my physical appearance, created a bitter cocktail of self-loathing that poisoned my confidence for years.

I have juggled the Absolute Narcissism and Crippling Self-Doubt sides of the Art diagram for most of my life, except the self-doubt circle is enormous and the other is tiny. You might think that graduating at the top of my class and getting into a prestigious university like Stanford would let me take a breath and say, Woo! I am very smart. Stupidly, it only brought more anxiety and self-doubt. Being at such a competitive school among *true geniuses*, I wondered how the heck I had gotten in. I stressed before every test and term paper. Would this be the trial that exposed me as a fraud, a mediocre mind? After four years of hard work and medium partying, I graduated with a double major, a high GPA, and low self-worth.

Like a golden retriever, my imposter syndrome faithfully followed me into the corporate world. I worked my insecure butt off, steadily got promoted, and became a strategy director in a big New York ad agency before the age of 30. My insecurities grew right alongside my salary. With a bigger title came more responsibility, more pressure. I couldn't shake the nagging fear that the next client meeting or new business pitch would expose my supposed strategy expertise as a few cards short of a full (PowerPoint) deck.

Do most adults secretly feel like they have no idea what they're doing? Asking for a friend.

Where did this constant, ambient insecurity come from? I received nothing but earnest praise from the outside world. My parents, teachers, coworkers, bosses, and clients all seemed to think I was a highly intelligent and fully-functioning human. I believed that *they* believed it, somehow. But I never fully believed it myself. My mother recently asked me the same question. "Where did you get this huge lack of self-confidence, this low self-esteem? We always told you how amazing you were."

Mumsie, I wish I knew. I think some of us come into this world with trauma from our past lives (see Chapter 23) and with a deep-seated drive to prove something to ourselves, not simply to others. My own standards were always impossibly high. No one will ever be as hard on me as I have been on myself—though I have thankfully eased up over the years. Making a careless mistake like calling someone by the wrong name used to gnaw at me for days. Now I am able to berate myself for a few minutes and then let it go, permanently.

I would give the same advice for curing imposter syndrome and inferiority complex as for curbing self-hate toward the person you see in the mirror. Start by simply loving the part of you that has these insecurities and self-doubts. Acknowledge them, let yourself feel them, notice how they weigh you down. Ask yourself whether they are serving you in any way. Motivating yourself to make positive changes from a place of self-love ("I am a good person who deserves more happiness") is a zillion times more likely to succeed than doing it from a place of self-loathing ("I am a loser who will probably fail"). The first one has the added benefit of being true.

Above all, realize that you are not alone. There are far more of us crippled by self-doubt than there are absolute narcissists. And somewhere in the middle is the beautiful art or music or stories you are meant to share with the world. Because channeling your own struggles and insecurities into something that helps others feel better about themselves—THAT is the highest form of genius.

5

EMPATHS ARE GETTING BAD ADVICE

Creating blocks and shields might keep pain out, but they also block out love

Ah, EMPATH. The latest buzzword in the realm of personal growth.

Are you highly attuned to the moods and emotions of others? Often overwhelmed by crowds? Do you feel drained after consoling a friend even though she feels much better after talking to YOU? Congratulations and condolences, you are probably an empath!

Being able to know what someone else is feeling might sound like a psychic superpower. But actually *feeling* another's emotions as if they were your own? That sounds more like a punishment if those emotions happen to be anger, sadness, or anxiety.

From a young age, I have hated scary movies and books. After consuming enough slasher films and Stephen King novels out of peer pressure and sheer curiosity, I realized something: these tales didn't make me feel scared. They made me feel *de-*

pressed. I would viscerally take on the pain of the characters. A general malaise over mankind's cruelty would linger for days.

Knowing it was fictional pain made it even worse. Wasn't there enough senseless suffering in the real world, I wondered, without having to manufacture more of it for sport? How did my friends watch the same movie and genuinely enjoy it?

I also convinced myself that I was an introvert, preferring my own company to that of others, especially large gatherings of others. Most people would simply exhaust me after enough time. By my twenties, I had perfected the stealthy Irish Goodbye at parties and feigned a few headaches to end unexpectedly lengthy dates. So when I first heard the term *empath* at a cacao ceremony in Guatemala at the impressionable age of 35, it was like meeting myself for the first time.

Holy Guacamole, I didn't actually hate people!

Deep down I actually longed for *more* social interaction, not less. But when you are unknowingly sipping up other people's emotional shit through an invisible straw, you are bound to feel pooped.

I also began to realize that some of us not only empath the pain of other humans, but of animals and plants. On a family trip to Sea World as a young girl, I remember feeling angry and sad during Shamu's star performance without knowing why. A killer whale's choreographed water dance should be captivating to a child, but I became visibly agitated. My parents thought it was an overreaction to the Texas heat. Decades later, I watched the documentary *Blackfish* and once again fought back tears, learning the cruelty behind these marine parks, the trauma of being captured in the wild and held in captivity.

There is a staggering amount of pain, anger, and sadness in the world. Relatedly, there are thousands of written guides and video tutorials on how to create energy shields, blocks, boundaries, and protective force fields around yourself if you are an energetically sensitive soul. A reputable psychology journal even suggests employing a jaguar to protect you from toxic energy. Presumably they mean calling forth this fierce animal spirit metaphorically, but now I want a real jaguar to ward off so-called energy vampires.

Many of us empaths have jerry-rigged our own protective blocks and shields and used them for years without consciously realizing it. Here are some of the methods I have unconsciously employed to shield myself from feeling other people's energetic pain (and undoubtedly some of my own)—in no particular order of effectiveness:

Wine. Work. Weed. Shopping. Comedy clubs. Sugar highs. Food binges. TV binges. Excessive exercise. Excessive solitude. Emotional distance (pushing them away). Physical distance (literal avoidance). Endless combinations of the above to distract, numb, or hide myself from the world.

It is perfectly understandable to prefer *not* feeling shitty and trying to avoid catching someone else's emotional flu. However, there are two major reasons why putting up blocks and shields is a terrible idea:

1. You will block yourself from feeling more *love*

LOST & FOUND

Generally, we feel emotions in and around our heart, the heart-center, heart chakra, or Anahata in Sanskrit traditions, which means "unhurt or unbeaten." Try to close yourself down from feeling hurt or otherwise unpleasant, and you also close yourself off from fully feeling the GOOD stuff. Love, joy, connection.

It would be like wearing a beekeeper suit full-time to avoid getting stung. Sure, it will keep the bees out. But it will also make it hard for non-bees to reach you with wonderful things like hugs and kisses. In other words, don't put a hazmat suit around your heart.

2. You will waste an amazing superpower

As an empath, you possess a powerful gift. You are a human pain-reliever. Ever wonder why strangers are always telling you deeply personal things on airplanes? Or why friends call you first when they are feeling down? People just seem to feel better around you. That's because you unknowingly act as a grounding rod for other people's pain and unprocessed traumas. I won't get into the fine print on how or why this happens, because quite frankly it's above my own level of spiritual and scientific understanding. But I have experienced it firsthand on both sides, as an empath easing others' pain, and as someone in pain surrounded by empaths.

If you don't put up energetic shields, you can help people more easily release pains and traumas they are ready to let go of—without ever saying a thing. Sounds sweet, right? Here is what to do instead of trying to block other people's energy:

ALLA POLSKY

Read the book, but don't eat the book

One of my spiritual teachers, whom you will formally meet in Chapter 9, recommends this simple yet advanced technique. The next time you are around someone giving off a negative vibe, or what you might specifically label as grief, sadness, fear, anger, guilt, complaining—instead of trying to deflect it, simply let yourself feel whatever it is making YOU feel. But do not make those feelings your own by creating a story around why you are feeling them.

You can read a book without eating it. We do it all the time with other people's words. You literally read a book and know that those are someone else's thoughts, not your own. Do the same thing with feelings. Don't make them yours, don't 'eat' them and hold on to them. Observe them without judgment, without labeling them as bad and wishing they would go away.

Okay, I'm feeling a sudden sadness right now. This is what it feels like in my body.

How will you know if it's your own pain or someone else's you are feeling? Let's say your mood changes suddenly with no explanation. If you are being fully present in that moment, rather than lost in your own thoughts, it will be very obvious.

My partner Herb had a striking experience of this while living in a spiritual community in Guatemala. He woke up one morning, meditated, and strolled off to yoga class. His mind was completely clear of chatter. He felt happy and present as he watched himself walk to class without a single thought. All of a sudden, he walked into what he could only describe as "a wall of sadness." There was no one else in sight, yet he could sense with absolute certainty that this sadness was not his own. As he continued up the stairs to the yoga studio and joined the other yogis waiting for class to start, a young woman burst into tears.

"I'm sorry, you guys. I just found out my aunt died," she told the group.

If Herb had not been fully present, he might have mistaken that sadness for his own, creating a story in his mind about why he suddenly felt down. Undoubtedly a sad memory from his past or a worry about the future would have popped into his head to help "explain" the shift in mood.

Ultimately, it doesn't really matter whether you are sensing your own pain or another's. You deal with both in exactly the same way. Feel it without judgment and be fully okay with its presence. That's when it transmutes, or moves. Notice it, be aware of it, but don't eat the book. Read its energy and then let it go as freely as it came in. Knowing that all feelings, no matter how blissful or painful, will eventually pass and be replaced by new feelings.

Instead of blocking your empath powers, try using them *more*. As you learn to be more present and fully open your heart, your empath Spidey Sense will get stronger and better at helping others—without hurting yourself in the process. Meditation is a great tool for being more present, as is connecting more to your passions, to nature, to other people. (Eckhart Tolle's *The Power of Now* is another great tool, referenced in more detail in later chapters.)

To reiterate the point, empaths are pain-relieving angels on this earth. Don't close down the gift that helps you heal others with your mere presence. Blocks and shields might keep some unwanted pain out, but they will also prevent love from coming in. And you are too amazing to not let yourself be fully loved.

PART II: FINDING PURPOSE

The term "finding yourself" makes me cringe a little. It sounds cheesy and self-indulgent. But at its core, finding yourself is about finding and following the path that makes you feel most alive, most you. The quest to find a meaningful life purpose tormented me for decades. Here are the learnings and experiences that finally steered me toward the path I was always meant to walk.

6

A ONE-STEP GUIDE TO FINDING YOURSELF

Step One: Unhide Yourself

I was painfully shy as a child. It was painful for me, anyway. I desperately wanted to come out of my shell, but that process would take many years.

Flashback to seven-year-old Alla. Midway through math class, she desperately has to pee. The number of class minutes left, minus the size of her bladder, equals a very embarrassing accident waiting to happen. But the solution is not so simple.

May I please be excused to use the bathroom? I knew how to say it the grown-up way in my native Russian.

But I am in a new school. In a new country. With a new language and new social norms. Just months before, my family had immigrated to the U.S. from Soviet Belarus.

My new American teacher had instructed me to simply say "Toilet" if I needed to go. I had already used this code word enough times in front of my new classmates to sense that it wasn't quite right. It drew snickers. It wasn't how a bright, mature second-grader would ask permission to pee. Especially not when it required interrupting the teacher's lesson to ask in front of the whole class.

So I remain silent. I wait so long that my bladder physically starts to hurt. The pain is so bad it makes me cry. Painfully shy. A classmate notices my tears and announces *Alla is crying* in perfect English and the teacher stops her lesson.

All eyes on me.

In retrospect, shouting TOILET! in the middle of class would have been less disruptive and humiliating than explaining my tears to a bilingual interpreter in the hallway. But this sort of counterproductive, hide-me-at-all-costs strategy would plague me for years.

What does this bladder trauma have to do with Finding Yourself?

Nothing, I just needed to get that story off my chest. Kidding! The truth is, I eventually conquered some of that childhood shyness, as many people do. Despite an ambient fear of attention and ridicule, I somehow went on to performing in dance and piano recitals, running for student government, working as a college campus tour guide, and eventually a corporate career that required public speaking in front of high profile CEOs and the occasional A-list celebrity.

Although I had conquered surface shyness—I could play a convincing extrovert who didn't hide from others—I was still hiding the real me, even from myself. I had buried her so deep that I didn't even know I was living a lie. Until the lie became unbearable. The nagging whisper that office life and PowerPoint decks were probably not my highest purpose turned into a soul-crushing scream I could no longer ignore.

So I quit the life I had worked for over a decade to build. I gave up my job and my apartment, sold all my furniture, and left my friends and family for a backpack and a passport.

> *Maybe the journey isn't so much about becoming anything. Maybe it's about unbecoming everything that isn't you, so you can be who you were meant to be in the first place.* —Paul Coelho

Like a movie character, I hoped that travel would fill the void I felt in my soul. That it could help me "find myself" and magically reveal my life purpose. Well, it didn't. Not in an instant, cinematic way, at least. But travel did gradually reshape my passions and redirect me toward the people and places that would completely change my life.

Finding Yourself is simply about Unhiding Yourself

It turns out that conquering shyness was just peeling back the first layer of who I really was. I could never have traveled solo around the world without that layer. But there were so many more layers of myself to unhide.

Unhiding my voice as a writer. The part of me that wrote purely for fun as a child, before she decided it wasn't good enough for others to read.

LOST & FOUND

Unhiding my passion for yoga. It would take six years from the moment I completed my yoga teacher certification to actually finding the courage to teach my first real class.

Unhiding my heart. After a painful breakup, it took ten years to fully open myself up to love. It was worth the inner work, and the wait.

I am still working on more layers. Good lord, there are many. But I'm not finding anything particularly new or surprising. These parts of me were there all along, simply buried under an avalanche of societal pressures and self-doubts.

Come out of your own closet

In *Light Is The New Black,* Rebecca Campbell talks about "coming out of the spiritual closet"—her personal shift from dimming her light and hiding her passion for spirituality to fully stepping into her power as a healer and intuitive guide for others. This path was coded into her soul's DNA from birth but she had denied or downplayed it for decades. Once she stopped hiding her gifts, her life completely transformed. She is now a bestselling author and helps thousands of people find and step into their own power.

Thankfully it's not rocket science. Finding yourself is as simple as unhiding your true self. Unhiding your gifts and passions. Sharing more of yourself with the world. I have dreamed of writing a book since around the time I first learned to hold a pencil. And I have feared it for almost as long. *Who am I to share THAT many words with others? Go ahead, write a cute little article or blog post. But a whole book? Who the hell do you think you are?*

ALLA POLSKY

Well, if you are reading these words, then my dream finally conquered my doubts. Published paper covers rock, or more specifically, my desire to hide under one.

I was painfully shy as a child because I was worried about what others thought of me, when I should have been far more concerned with what I thought of myself. Not only is the latter more important, it's also a considerably more fun way to exist. Am I living the life I would want for myself? Am I saying and doing things that would make ME happy and proud? Ultimately, we only have to answer to ourselves.

I would be lying if I said I was done with the unhiding process. My imposter syndrome with its *I'm not good enough*'s still flares up on occasion. I am still my own harshest critic. But I am also my own biggest fan. It feels contradictory and confusing but also refreshingly freeing. Much like finally getting to pee after needlessly holding it in for a painfully long time.

7

A Reason You Don't Know Your Purpose Yet

You might be a Generalist. It's sexier than it sounds.

My cousin Alan started dancing at age 6 and never stopped. Today he is a pro dancer on the hit show *Dancing With The Stars*. Not just any pro dancer, but the reigning champion (at the time of writing).

Now, if you had asked 6-year-old Alan what he wanted to be when he grew up, would he have said "I want to dance shirtless for millions of people and post Instagram stories of spooning in bed with my Mirrorball Trophy"?

Well, maybe. Alan *has* known almost unwaveringly that his life purpose revolves around entertaining people. To dance and perform and make people smile.

I took dance classes as a kid, too. I wasn't half bad. But I didn't specialize in dance. I also took piano lessons. And spent countless hours drawing portraits. Oh, and also writing poetry. Now as an adult, my interests are just as diverse but considerably more expensive. Travel. Scuba diving. Photography.

Alan is an undeniable success story. I'm a bit of a lost soul.

ALLA POLSKY

Through hard work and laser focus, Alan followed his passion all the way to a fulfilling purpose and a pretty paycheck. Me? Even at the age of forty, I am still not entirely sure what I want to do with my life. Thus far my paid work and leisure interests have rarely intersected. My advertising strategy work pays for my passions. It is not, in itself, a passion.

And what of that other p-word, Purpose? I have never felt a calling to do one thing in particular above all others. At least not for a lengthy stretch of time. *Follow your dream* is a daunting instruction to follow even if you manage to pinpoint exactly what that dream is. But what if you don't have one singular 'dream'? Mine is a messy smorgasbord of smaller, disconnected dreams.

I dream of (in no particular order): Publishing a book (maybe this one). Sailing around the world. Pitching a travel show to Netflix (perhaps about sailing). Scuba diving to find a seven-inch Megalodon shark tooth (they exist). Hosting cacao ceremonies on every continent (you're all invited). Being a source of joy and healing for others, together with my partner.

I'm not stage-five-clinger attached to any of these dreams except maybe the last one. I have been knocked sideways by enough curveballs over the years to fully appreciate the truth in the saying, "If you want to make God laugh, tell Him your plans." That said, I am not passively surrendering to his cosmic whims, either. I am working toward these dreams while leaving space for life to surprise or redirect me.

When Herb was young, his dream was to open a martial arts dojo and train students the way his instructors had taught him for many years and thousands of hours. It wasn't even a dream so much as a deep knowing and strong calling. "I could not imagine a reality where the martial arts were not a big part of my life," he said of his mindset at the time. But within a few years, reality shifted. He no longer felt drawn to the ego-centered energy of being a tough guy or inflicting pain. Instead he gravitated toward the heart-centered energy of meditation and helping others heal their pain. By the look of Herb's resume, his career path has reincarnated a dozen ways since the dojo days. Oil field worker, nightclub bouncer, software developer, meditation teacher, world traveler, hostel owner, clinical hypnotherapist. Yet an underlying healing energy has steadily steered him away from egocentric roles and toward being of greater service to others.

On a societal level, we still romanticize the pursuit of a lifelong, single-minded purpose that borders on obsession. Winning an Olympic medal. Visiting every country in the world. Building a billion-dollar app. But having multiple, shapeshifting purposes can be just as exciting—and infinitely more common—than one singular, laser-focused, mother-of-all-purposes.

Maybe I'm just trying to post-rationalize my messy smorgasbord, but I know I'm not solely meant to be a writer. Nor a yoga teacher. Nor even a marine paleontologist who scours the world's oceans in search of hand-sized Megalodon teeth that shredded their last meal over 3 million years ago. (My latest hobby is admittedly the most random but arguably the most awesome.)

Wait. Why was I telling you this?

Oh, right. It took me *decades* of feeling lame and purposeless to realize that my wide range of interests and skills is not only a strength, but a purpose in itself. Perhaps these words will help accelerate someone else's realization.

Why having range is all the rage

At the start of the pandemic, having mastered the baking of banana bread and looking for new lockdown-friendly distractions, I read David Epstein's bestseller *Range: Why Generalists Triumph In A Specialized World.*

It was like chicken soup for my lost, wandering soul.

A fellow meanderer, Epstein examined the world's most successful athletes, artists, musicians, inventors, scientists and all-around MVPs of the human race.

He discovered that in most fields—especially those that are complex and unpredictable—generalists, not specialists, are primed to excel. "Generalists often find their path late, and they juggle many interests rather than focusing on one. They're also more creative, more agile, and able to make connections their more specialized peers can't see."[3]

As it turns out, frequent fail-ers, quitters and pivot-ers often end up with deeply fulfilling lives and careers. While specialists are busy burrowing into one single field or interest, generalists bounce around amassing breadth instead of depth. They then become innovative dot connectors between seemingly disparate things, creating new mash-ups or spotting surprising parallels only visible from their unique vantage point.

Perhaps I will combine my passions for yoga and scuba diving to create custom yoga classes and breathing exercises specifically for divers. Or I shall write a highly relatable novel about a generalist mermaid who befriends a specialized megalodon shark because she is clever and creative enough to not get eaten.

Either way, my passion compass keeps pointing me in multiple directions for a reason. I'm not sure what that reason is yet, but some of the dots are already starting to connect in purposeful ways (this book being one example).

Preventing passion paralysis

For those of us with multiple interests, hobbies, and passions, there is the pesky issue of paralysis. It pops up as uncertainty in career path and life purpose but also annoyingly during leisure time. If I have an hour free to do anything I want before a scheduled meeting: "Ooh, let's see. I could play the ukulele for a bit. No wait, I haven't touched the piano in weeks. Then again, I haven't touched my drawing pencils in *months*. Oh, but more recently, I skipped yoga this morning. A self-guided, wacky flow would be fun *and* good for my health..."

After twenty minutes of trying to decide what type of fun I should have right now, I give up completely because decision-making is not fun at all. Instead I spend a half hour returning messages on my phone.

How shall a generalist prevent such passion paralysis? The key is in that dirty little s-word, *should*. When I start asking myself what type of fun I should select right now, I am asking the wrong body part. The should's live in the head. The true answer to what you really want to do right now generally lives in the body, as the next chapter on intuition will explore.

My friend Kerin keeps the inside of her car immaculately clean. If you open the trunk against her wishes, however, you will get a cluttered surprise. She lovingly refers to her trunk as "The Land of Lost Hobbies." Over the years it has amassed an impressive assortment of recreational and sporting goods like tennis rackets, rollerblades, frisbees, cycling gear, and camping equipment. All the activities her head had at one point suggested she *should* get into, until her heart overruled the new hobby and banished it into the trunk graveyard forever.

Your five-year-old self never asked its brain what it wanted to play, nor felt the need to make a strategic list of entertainment options. Your little heart instinctively knew exactly what it felt like doing in any given moment—whether drawing or dancing or giving yourself a haircut with bangs (like my sister at age 5)—and simply did it. Only as adults do we learn the word *should* and mistakenly apply it to our hobbies and free time.

If you find yourself paralyzed by your plethora of passions or find your energy scattered across too many pursuits to make any real progress in one, simply ask your inner child what it finds most exciting right now. It always knows. *That's* the passion to pour your heart into today. I am not saying to use perpetual playtime as an excuse not to accomplish anything productive. Your inner child knows exactly what it wants to do, and your outer adult (ideally) knows how to channel that joy into something that will help others and/or help you make money, whether right now or eventually.

LOST & FOUND

One last P

Because alliteration is awesome: Permission! Recognizing our passions and realizing we may have more than one purpose is only a triumph if we give ourselves permission to simply *enjoy* them. Permission to take the pressure off from "succeeding" at any of it. Permission to not even care if it's a purpose or a passion or a passing phase.

There's a fascinating documentary called *First Contact* starring a man named Darryl Anka, who (claims he) has been a channel for an extraterrestrial named Bashar for the last few decades. He travels the world (and presumably the universe) speaking in packed venues about the importance of pursuing your passion right here on Earth.

Whether you believe in alien encounters is refreshingly besides the point. "We have no need for you to believe in us," Bashar the E.T. says. "We are here to assist you in believing in yourselves." He also says, "If you can't figure out your purpose, figure out your passion. For your passion will lead you directly to your purpose."

I would only add one small 's' to this otherwise perfect cosmic wisdom. If you can't figure out your purpose, figure out your passion(s). Plural or singular. The world needs us generalists just as much as it needs specialists.

Whether your own purpose(s) ultimately involves feeling more fulfilled in your current career, or turning your passions into paychecks, or simply experiencing this fleeting lifetime more passionately in each moment—give yourself permission to enjoy the pursuit itself. Permission to approach life like

ALLA POLSKY

a waking dream where reality meets magic and anything is possible. It starts to feel a lot like my cousin Alan greeting his Mirrorball Trophy with a galaxy-sized grin on national TV.

8

A MESSAGE FROM YOUR INTUITION

It's tired of being misunderstood

"So, how did you end up in Mexico?"

While living in a hostel in Mexico packed with travelers from all over the world, I met many with slightly different versions of the same general answer to this question.

"I just had a feeling I needed to go there. It made no rational sense. My family even tried to talk me out of it, but I just had this hunch that it was the right thing to do."

Many of these solo travelers did not know a soul in Mexico, had never been before, and needed to cross a large ocean to get there. One young woman named Julija from Lithuania, who stayed at our hostel for three months, recalled her journey to me:

"I always had a long list of countries I wanted to visit, and Mexico was never on the list. While living in my hometown, I fell into a deep depression, and Mexico suddenly started popping into my head. Each time I tried to ignore it, the message came back stronger. It seemed crazy to my rational mind. What would I do in Mexico? How could I afford it if I quit my job in Lithuania? One day as I was walking through the old town and wrestling with these questions, a Frida Kahlo book caught my attention in a store window. It was practically shouting at me. Mexico was shouting at me."

Eventually that intuitive feeling got so strong that Julija gave in. She found a one-way flight to Mexico and checked her bank balance. She had just enough funds to cover the flight. This didn't scare her. On the contrary, she took it as another sign that she was meant to go.

Upon arriving in Mexico, she still had no idea why she was called there. She began volunteering at a school for yoga and meditation. But the school was forced to close when the pandemic started. She then followed her inner compass into the jungle. "I had heard about a peaceful place where you can sleep in a tent and be in nature. I'd always wanted to do something like that." When she arrived, she realized it was a healing center that specialized in ayahuasca ceremonies.

"That was the real start of my own healing journey," Julija told me. "I met my soul family there. I participated in numerous ceremonies. During my very first one, Mother Ayahuasca told me, *Remember all those signs to come to Mexico? This is why. So you could find the medicine and begin healing.*

Then Julija's story got even crazier, at least to the rational mind. Ten years prior, she had stumbled upon a beautiful image online. It was vibrant, spiritual, vaguely psychedelic. It touched her so deeply that she printed it out and hung it on her vision board for years. She even made a wallet-size version to carry in her phone case. It was always with her, the one image she took along on her travels to Mexico.

LOST & FOUND

Shortly after connecting with the plant medicine of ayahuasca, she had the opportunity to sit with a shaman visiting from Peru. He was a gifted artist as well as a gifted healer. After meeting him, she Googled his artwork and was shocked to see her own favorite talisman. This shaman was the creator of the image she had carried around for years! The image that inspired and comforted her on many levels.

It seems the universe had long been calling Julija to the other side of the world. She followed her intuition, as random and strange as it sounded at the time, and found close friendships, meaningful work, and deep healing in Mexico.

My friend's transformative experience is far from an outlier. I know countless travelers with similar tales of limited funds and that little hunch to get on a plane. Some have met serious romantic partners on their travels. Others have met business partners and formed exciting new ventures. Most have transformed their lives in lasting ways.

Intuition is not a thought or a feeling

It is hard to fully capture the concept of intuition in words. To truly grasp it you must experience it firsthand, either by following a hunch on something, or wishing that you had, in retrospect.

We have many names for that little hunch. Intuition. Sixth Sense. Spidey Sense. Instinct. Gut feeling. Inner knowing. Inner wisdom. That inner wisdom does not originate in the mind nor is it an emotion, even though we sometimes refer to intuition as a gut feeling.

Our thoughts and feelings are constantly changing. You feel happy in one moment and sad in another. A single thought, like an upsetting memory from the past or an anxious worry about the future, can instantly shift your mood from upbeat to down.

Intuition is far more consistent. It does not change from moment to moment or send you mixed messages like your thoughts and feelings. Intuition is that nagging inner voice, that little hunch, that just won't go away. And it's a hunch that often makes zero sense to your rational mind.

There is no 'good reason' to follow it. It might even sound nuts. Your own mind, and your loved ones, may try to talk you out of it, but that little hunch will continue to nag you until you do something about it, as Julija learned in Lithuania.

Years ago my partner Herb did some healing energy work for a friend of a friend. While working with this woman, he had a strange sudden instinct to tug on her left ear. His rational mind immediately intervened.

No way. I'm not doing that. That is weird even for me. This woman will sit up and slap me if I do that.

But that little hunch persisted until his hands gave in. He tugged on her ear as his intuition instructed. The woman let out a deep sigh and relaxed twice as deeply as before the ear tugging.

After the session, she exclaimed, "That was AMAZING! How did you know to do that?" "Do what?" he asked. "I felt this huge blockage on the left side of my face, and when you pulled on my ear, it instantly cleared."

Herb's thoughts and feelings had both said, *That's a crazy idea—don't do it!* If he had let his intuition be overruled by the resistance from his rational mind and the fearful feeling of doing something weird, this woman would not have received the deeper healing she needed.

You can trust it the easy way or the hard way

Intuition is not for our reasoning mind to figure out. It comes from a deeper intelligence within. It is your higher self invisibly guiding you toward your brightest potential in this life.

We have all had (and regrettably ignored) a hunch that someone was wrong for us as a prospective mate, a prospective boss, or even as a friend. As one woman lamented in a Facebook group, "My intuition or 'gut' is nearly always right, which I hate sometimes."

Sometimes we learn to listen the hard way, after a few wrong turns. But ask anyone who has found their soulmate about how it happened. "I just *knew*," they say. Intuition is easy and effortless, if you allow it to be.

I didn't allow it to be easy for years. I kept forcing myself to stay in New York City and continue the dismal dating scene and stressful career path I had stumbled into right out of college. Deep down I knew it was making me miserable and not feeding my soul, but change is scary, so I stayed. Until one October morning when my landlord shoved a standard lease renewal under the door of my little studio apartment. I suddenly *just knew* that there was no way I could sign that lease for another year. I was finally ready to listen to my intuition. *It's time to leave New York*, it said.

When I told my landlord the big news, he informed me that I had a few weeks to vacate. My rational mind took a few moments to panic. What had I done? Where would I go? But my intuition whispered, *You got this. It doesn't matter where you go, only that you leave here.* I started putting my New York City exodus in motion so quickly that I even forgot to mention it to close friends until several days later.

I gave notice at my job. I sold all my furniture. I booked a one-way flight to Costa Rica for a yoga teacher training in the jungle (more on that in Chapter 12).

None of these steps were as hard as the first one: breaking years of inertia by deciding not to renew my apartment lease. The universe made the rest easy. A woman came to look at one piece of furniture and decided to buy everything I had for sale—even my digital piano. I snagged one of the last remaining spots in the yoga teacher training. The last-minute flight to Costa Rica was surprisingly affordable.

You know you're on the right track when the obstacles seem to fall away. The universe is on your side.

Intuition is instant, in-the-moment guidance

Years ago I made a rookie travel mistake: I booked a one-way flight to the Philippines without any proof of return or onward travel out of the country. Sometimes no one asks to see the proof, but on this 15-hour redeye out of Los Angeles, they were sticklers for the rules. The airline refused to issue my boarding pass until I could show proof of a flight out.

LOST & FOUND

I had fifteen minutes to book travel to somewhere, anywhere, out of the Philippines, before the check-in counter closed. I quickly searched for cheap flights on my phone. Manila to Literally Anywhere in the World (sites like Skyscanner have this handy feature).

For some reason, a flight to Sri Lanka caught my eye. I had never been there nor known anyone who had. I could barely locate the country on a map. But that particular flight might as well have had flashing lights around it.

I didn't have time to ponder WHY my intuition was sending me there, nor did my rational mind have time to talk me out of it. So I booked the flight. It felt random even for me, a gal who had spent years bouncing around the world in no particular order.

Today when people ask me if I have a favorite country out of dozens visited, I say Sri Lanka. And the giant smile on my face confirms that it's true. I could write a whole separate book on why it's a magical place. The scenic train rides. The elephant sanctuaries. The sunrise hikes to ancient temples and the surfing lessons atop emerald waves.

But it's the personal synchronicities I had with local people and fellow travelers that I needed most. They reminded me to believe in magic again. To renew my faith in the universe having my back, at a time when I had been feeling out of sync and disconnected from others.

Thank you, intuition. And a special thank you to the strict airline agent at LAX for the cosmic nudge in the right direction.

ALLA POLSKY

Intuition is more needed than ever

Modern life requires so many decisions from us, and from a seemingly infinite list of options. Some are trivial but nonetheless draining on our energy, like picking a movie to watch or deciding what to order for dinner. Some are medium-stress, like deciding where to travel for a big trip. Others are huge and potentially life-changing, like choosing a life partner, a university, a career path.

All of these decisions were easier in the olden days. Long before delivery apps, your dining options were limited to whatever you were able to grow, kill, or barter that day. Before Tinder, your mating prospects were left to the geography gods or the village matchmaker. I am not suggesting life was easier back then, but decision-making must have been a breeze. At least until 1946, when things became perplexing enough to necessitate the invention of the Magic 8-Ball.

With the endless options of today's world, learning how to hear and trust our intuition is more important than ever. It's also more reliable than asking a plastic ball.

Psychologist Barry Schwartz has uncovered the paradox of choice through extensive research: being faced with too many options actually makes us stressed, less able to make a decision, and less satisfied with our choice after we make one.[4] The sweet spot seems to be between 8 and 15 options for optimally picking out most things, like a new car to buy or a movie to watch. Ever wonder why Netflix only features a small, repetitive set of movies despite having a library of thousands? If they overwhelm you with too many titles, you will likely give up and go play with your Magic 8-Ball instead.

LOST & FOUND

Research has also shown that we tend to make better decisions when we have to pee. Yes, you read that right. There is actual science behind this.

Mirjam Tuk and her colleagues at the University of Twente in the Netherlands compared the decision-making abilities of people with full versus empty bladders.[5] Please sign me up for the empty bladder control group. But the selfless water chuggers made a crucial contribution to science: "You seem to make better decisions when you have a full bladder," Tuk says.

Participants were asked to make a series of choices, each between receiving a small, immediate reward or a larger, delayed reward. For example, get $16 tomorrow or $30 in 35 days. The people with full bladders were better at holding out for the larger reward later. In other words, they were better at acting in their higher good, their fuller (pun intended) potential.

My own intuition tells me that people with full bladders suspended their thinking brain and acted on pure instinct. Intuition is immediate, in-the-moment knowing. And when your bladder is about to burst, time is of the essence. The instinctive decision turned out to be the better one.

Are some people more intuitive than others?

Bestselling author and spiritual teacher Sonia Choquette says that every single person is innately intuitive, but many of us doubt or deny our ability.[6]

Our society perpetuates the misconception that intuition is born rather than bred. *Women's intuition* suggests that half the population is innately more intuitive than the other half. Most self-proclaimed psychics and clairvoyants tend to be women.

And then there are mystics, shamans, and gurus—people we hope will magically know more than we do about our own lives. When I first met the cacao shaman you will formally meet in the next chapter, I was blown away by how empathically intuitive he was about my life struggles. From the moment we made eye contact, I knew I couldn't bullshit this man or hide my true self from him. He saw right through my shields and helped me release some deep, lifelong pain.

After working with him for several weeks, he confessed that for the first half of his life, he was completely closed off from his gifts. "I didn't even know how to tune into what *I* was feeling, let alone what others were feeling. I was a dense jerk asshole!" If this incredibly intuitive healer started out so far from this path, I realized that there is ample hope and ample time for all of us to step into our power and connect with our true calling.

Intuition is like any ability. The more you practice it and make it a priority in your life, the better you will become. We are all born with the wiring for it, but through years of social conditioning, we become blind to it. We turn the decision-making power over to our rational thinking brain—especially if we were raised in a secular Western culture that values the intellectual mind above all.

I think, therefore I am...confused?

LOST & FOUND

Ever since René Descartes helped usher in the era ambitiously named The Enlightenment, millions of minds around the world have been taught his terribly misleading phrase.

The Enlightenment in Europe championed the rational thinking mind. Science split from spirituality. Everything that could be tested and observed, versus that which relied on faith or pure instinct. And yet, the owner of the world's most famous mind, Albert Einstein, was a big fan of intuition:

> *The intuitive mind is a sacred gift and the rational mind is a faithful servant.*

There is some debate about the author of this next statement (either Einstein or Bob Samples), but that doesn't make it any less true:

> *We have created a society that honors the servant and has forgotten the gift.*

Choquette explains in an interview that our logic brain has been trained to attack our intuition, and what it needs to do is be retrained to support our intuition. If only Einstein had left a formula for this.

Different types of intuition

Choquette has a great traffic light analogy[7] for explaining the different types of intuition we all have.

Red light intuition is our warning system, which lives in the gut. When something just seems dangerous, unsafe or simply like it's a bad idea, our intuition is trying to protect us. As a woman who has traveled solo around the world, I use my red light intuition to literally keep me alive. There were times I just got a bad vibe about walking down a certain street or staying in a certain guesthouse.

Green light intuition is our motivator or cheerleader. It lives in the heart. That inner knowing when something is a good idea, or someone is a good person for us to connect with. You sense a green light to take action. Even if others or your own rational mind says it's a crazy idea, trust that inner knowing. Most trailblazers in science, technology and business are highly attuned to the green light. The Wright Brothers. Nicola Tesla. When society laughed or doubted their ideas, they persisted. And our world was transformed because they followed their heart.

Yellow light intuition is our pause button. Sometimes your intuition says it's not quite time to take action yet. Perhaps new information or opportunities are yet to be revealed.

Spiritual teacher and author Matt Kahn has a powerful way of framing the yellow light: "Everyone is 100% intuitive about the things they need to know. If there are things that aren't known, it simply reminds you what doesn't need to be known at this time. While so many beings work diligently on developing their intuition, it is done in an attempt to know more than each moment provides.

"No matter how crystal clear your intuition becomes, you will never see or know more than is meant to be revealed.

In fact, without even working on honing the power of your intuition, you will always know exactly where to go and what to do at the moment you are meant to move." (A post from Matt Kahn's public Facebook page: May 1, 2015.)

Ways to strengthen your intuition radar

First, acknowledge that this is a superpower you were born with. Your gift simply needs to be charged to full strength by your confidence in its existence and your willingness to actually hear it. At its core, toning our intuitive muscles merely requires us to become better listeners. To practice listening to our inner guidance with our whole being instead of with our ears and chatty thinking mind.

Do things that quiet the mind and put you more in tune with your body so that you can hear the wisest part of you. Meditate. Spend time in nature. Do what brings you joy and puts you in an ultra-present flow state. For some that's creating art, for others it's dancing or baking or playing a musical instrument.

I need to clear my head. We say this when we feel stuck or don't know what to do about something. It's easy to say and hard to follow. We have been so conditioned to use our mind to solve the very problems it created. But if you can silence the chatter long enough to hear your intuition, it will be well worth the effort.

Above all, be patient with yourself. Intuition isn't always available on demand. Knowings don't come just because you want them right now. I get mine when I least expect them.

When I surrender to the fact that *not* knowing my next step *yet* must be in my highest good.

When intuition does call, have the courage to answer

This may come as a surprise, given what you are currently reading: I don't really like to write. Often it takes Herculean mental effort to find the right words, and so my mind keeps wandering off to all the easier, more enjoyable things I could be doing instead.

I wrote a crappy first draft of this chapter and then put off editing it for days by distracting myself with easier, more enjoyable activities like watching multiple seasons of *Vikings*. My intuition politely said, *Okay, Alla, you've had your fun. It's time to write now.*

I politely told my intuition to take a hike, closed my laptop, and opened a book about lucid dreaming. Reading is a responsible warm-up to writing, I reasoned with myself. But deep down I knew I was stalling on doing the harder thing, the better thing for my highest good.

My mind didn't like the guilty feeling that ensued, so it offered a mental negotiation: *If I am truly supposed to be writing about intuition right now, let this lucid dreaming book send me a sign.*

On a rational level, I figured the chances of this were quite small, and I could settle in for a reading marathon. About ten pages in, the author shifted from lucid dreaming to the power of intuition.

"Oh, come on!" I literally said out loud. But I got the message. No more stalling. I closed the book and began editing this piece. It proved to be easier and more enjoyable than I expected. (Not as easy as watching *Vikings*, but surprisingly close.)

The hardest part about intuition isn't hearing it. It's actually following it. Going against your thoughts of doubt and feelings of fear, and going toward the direction of your highest, brightest future.

It won't always be easy, but it will make your life better than your rational, smartypants brain could ever imagine. Trust the part of you that already knows this to be true.

9

A School For Getting Out Of Your Own Way

Heart-opening wisdom from Guatemala's 'Chocolate Shaman'

What the heck is a cacao ceremony?

Step off a water taxi onto the small public dock in San Marcos La Laguna, and it's only a matter of time before the term *cacao ceremony* enters your consciousness.

San Marcos is one of the sleepier Mayan villages hugging the shore of Guatemala's stunning Lake Atitlán. Surrounded by volcanoes, some still active, the lake is a sacred site for the Maya people, a hashtag heaven for Instagrammers, and a travel magnet for backpackers with yoga mats.

I belong to the last group.

I don't know a soul out here, but my own having been flagged as lost and directionless, I arrive ready to meditate. Or at least stare quietly at volcanoes.

Instead I find myself staring at two cryptic words. The town's cozy main street beckons with colorful flyers for cacao ceremonies. They manage to stand out even amidst posterized competition for "soul retrieval" treatments and magic mushroom growing workshops. (Toto, I don't think we're anywhere near Kansas.)

Cacao next catches my eye on the village white board of daily events, scribbled in black Sharpie: *Cacao Ceremony & Ecstatic Dance.*

I am still weighing the prospect of dancing ecstatically when it appears yet again, audibly this time. Waiting for my veggie burrito lunch order, I begin chatting with a fellow traveler at the next table. Already in town for a few weeks, he replies decisively when I ask for recreational recos in this mysterious hippie hideaway.

"Let's see, what day is it? Friday? Check out Keith's on Sunday."

"Keith's what?"

"Cacao ceremony."

Okay, the only part of that I got is *Sunday*. This Keith character must be locally renown, doubling as a person and an address.

But why is everyone acting like *cacao ceremony* is the most self-explanatory phrase in the world, like it's *wine tasting*?

At first I mistake the vagueness for hippie arrogance—you know, to keep any half-hearted soul-seekers in the dark. Weed out the weekday vegetarians. But I would soon learn that the mystery was without malice. Cacao ceremonies are, quite simply, hard to articulate.

And yet I feel compelled to try. During my first stay in San Marcos, I would end up spending three Sundays on Keith's porch—about twenty hours total—and the things I learned yearn to be overshared with strangers. Prior to my first cacao ceremony, here is what little intel I had gathered:

1. You drink cacao—whatever that is, exactly. Sounds vaguely like hot cocoa. Is cacao just an exotic way of saying hot chocolate?

2. You feel...*different*—cacao gives you a high that people describe as a "heart opener." At this point all I feel is a "head scratcher."

3. You do *ceremonial things*. Whether this involves ritual animal sacrifice or chanting around a fire, I couldn't yet say.

The Porch

San Marcos is a tiny town, so Keith's house proves much easier to find than any workable description for cacao ceremony. I arrive early, pay the 200 Quetzal ($26 US) fee for first-timers—it's half for subsequent visits—and find a spot on the covered porch as its floor pillows begin to fill up with butts.

Thirty of us sit barefoot in loose rows facing the house. Our ages span five decades, and from the accents, at least a dozen countries. A guy who has clearly been here before remarks that our crowd is large for this time of year, the rainy low season, but would be considered paltry in high season, when up to fifty cacao enthusiasts will cram onto this cozy porch twice a week.

The ambient chatter wanes as our leader emerges from a doorway of hanging beads. He welcomes us and takes his ceremonial seat, a foldable camping chair, as his cat Squeaky jumps into his lap for a ceremonial nap.

The Man

Keith Wilson is an American ex-pat who has lived in Guatemala since 2003. He has the gravitas and hair of Gandalf the Grey, the bluntness of Tony Robbins, and the sharp observational wit of George Carlin (minus the cynicism).

Keith is the Chocolate Shaman, a nickname bestowed by his students when he began using cacao as a facilitator in his healing work. Keith introduces a woman named Barbara, whole-heartedly as his sweetheart, and half-jokingly as the Cacao Whisperer. Together they make a chocolate power couple, hosting these gatherings and producing a high quality "ceremonial grade" cacao under the label *Keith's Cacao*. It is served on tap at local restaurants and available for purchase online, servicing Keith's international tribe of cacao disciples.

Barbara passes around a tray of reusable plastic cups half-filled with a warm brown liquid while Keith rattles off some health advisories.

The Plan

"First I'm going to tell you why you *shouldn't* drink this. Your heart rate will rise by 20%. Don't climb a mountain today if you have high blood pressure. Don't drink it if you're on high doses of an anti-depressant. And if you're a dog, cat, parrot or horse, this stuff will kill you." (Luckily, Squeaky doesn't seem to care for cacao.)

After a brief intention-setting, we raise our cups in gratitude to the Cacao Spirit. Then it's down the hatch.

Cacao is bitter. Nature's built-in portion control. It's like drinking pure 100% dark chocolate. Optional sweeteners are passed around for those of us with tainted taste buds from years of sugary sodas and mocha Frappuccinos. While we wait for the effects to fully kick in—forty minutes, we're told—Keith launches into the most fascinating monologue of all time. Or maybe my cacao buzz has simply kicked in early.

The Monologue

"This is a school," he says. "A school for how to get out of your own way. It's a school for healers, teachers, energy workers, creators, artists, manifesters. But we don't teach techniques in those subjects. Because you don't need it. Everything is already inside, ready to roll. All you need to do is get out of your own way. And you're all absolutely terrified to do that."

Standing In My Own Way could be the title of my autobiography. The man has my attention.

"You're in a war between your head and your heart," he continues. "But you're all a bunch of wizards. Magicians. Absolutely magic people, hiding in the closet. So my job is to threaten you with the scariest thing on Earth: who you really are."

Wait. Who *am* I? Cue the existential crisis I seem to have fortnightly these days. Keith offers an answer, but it only brings up more questions. "You are not a human being. You are a being of light...that chose an expression in a human body. For whatever you came here to do."

The Chocolate Shaman is circling a question that has nagged me for decades. *What's my damn purpose in this life?* Is there something specific I should be *doing* in this pesky human body that I apparently chose? (And why didn't I choose one bearing closer resemblance to a Brazilian supermodel?)

Keith resumes his spiritual pep-talk with the news that we are all expert healers already. Which is handy, because the world is going to need plenty of those in the coming years. A lot of people will be in pain, dealing with personal dramas and the dismal state of the planet. He cites the exceedingly extreme weather, the downplaying of the global damage from Fukushima, the imminent collapse of the euro and eventually the world market, and whatever shady shenanigans are going on in Antarctica. (A recent surge in scientists to the area, plus the installment of enough fiber-optic cable to only make sense "if the penguins are getting online.")

I nod instinctively. Conspiracy theories aside, one doesn't need psychic abilities to suspect that Mother Nature is agitated or that the global economy is fragile or that today's governments keep enormous secrets from the public. (This gathering took place in Pre-Pandemic Times, circa 2018.)

Our modern Nostradamus warns that things are going to get a lot worse before they get better (Oh, hey, 2020)—but we have the power to ease our own suffering and that of others.

Well, phew. How?

"You can take the hard bus, the easy bus, or the magic bus. Which one do you want?"

ALLA POLSKY

Jesus, Mary and Chocolate, give us the magic bus!

Keith must have sensed the group's cacao buzz peaking, because he abruptly shifts gears from monologue to guided meditation.

The Meditation

"Okay, close your eyes. This stupid-simple meditation called Glow takes about a second and a half to activate. [Dramatic pause] Ask the smile in your heart to find you. And as it does, *smile*. Let that energy spread over your face. If you're having trouble smiling because you've been taught that meditation is a serious pursuit, I'll come over and tickle you! [Scattered laughs] If you're willing to smile, you'll notice that you are radiating energy. Gently glowing. Yes? Feel it?"

I feel myself nodding, eyes closed. Over the next few minutes, I feel a lightness I have never quite felt before. Ca-cao! My heart seems doubled in size. Heart opener, indeed. It's an effortless, natural high that eclipses what I've felt in far lengthier meditations and intense yoga classes.

Keith concludes with the practical applications of Glowing. "When you're crossing borders, dealing with cranky customs agents, *Go to Glow*. Talking to customer service reps on the phone? Go to Glow. Hanging out with a friend who's in blame-or-complain mode? Go to Glow. Watch their energy shift almost immediately."

If this were a late-night infomercial, I'd have already picked up the phone and dialed 1–800-GLOW. The next testimonial would double my order. Keith's former student went to Glow at an airline check-in counter and got upgraded to first class for no apparent reason. (The full meditation can be found on Keith's YouTube page by searching "the chocolate shaman".)

Over the next few hours, it's a spiritual smorgasbord of talking to our higher selves, healing childhood traumas, and learning how to jump between parallel universes. Just your average Sunday at the Church of the Holy Cacao Spirit.

The Chocolate

Keith says cacao is a doorway to connect more easily and deeply to whatever you want, be it other people or your inner self or an experience. But doorways don't cross themselves. If you expect to be passively taken somewhere, the way psychedelic drugs take you on a trip, you'll be disappointed.

Step through the door, and the rewards are compelling. More clarity and focus for writers, artists, programmers. Enhanced productivity and collaboration for corporate teams. Deeper intimacy with loved ones. Cacao can be a creative muse or a couples therapist. The benefits listed on Keith's blog make it sound like a multi-vitamin for your higher self: there's almost nothing in your life it won't make better.

I suspect Silicon Valley will soon tire of chugging bulletproof coffee, popping Adderall and micro-dosing LSD—and switch to cacao to maintain a competitive edge. I have already found it more brain-waking than my morning coffee and more socially lubricating than a glass of wine. Several travelers I meet at Keith's soon become dear friends and one becomes my soulmate. (I meet Herb through Keith's ceremonies, although we will not start dating for several years, as Chapter 1 explained.)

The word chocolate itself spawned from *xocolatl*, an ancient Aztec word for a bitter drink brewed from cacao beans. A drink thought to have divine powers, whose metaphorical meaning was "heart blood." The ancient Mayans and Aztecs often get credited as the world's first cacao drinkers, but the use of this heart-opening medicine plant can be traced back over 5,000 years.

So liquid love was consumed long before it turned into solid heart-shaped candy exchanged on Valentines Day. In the centuries between xocolatl and Hershey's, cacao got grossly diluted and sugary—and the link to love went from spiritual to commercial. Keith is resuscitating an ancient tool to help us connect more deeply to ourselves, to each other, and to the divinity in everything. The scientific genus name for the cacao plant? Theobroma, or Food of the Gods.

I am clearly drinking the chocolate Kool-Aid at this point, literally and figuratively. But does one have to gnaw on a solid block of pure cacao or drink a ceremonial dose of ancient heart-blood in order to reach a heightened state? Of course not.

The Secret

"If you want to be spiritual, here's what you have to do," Keith says. "Have more fun. More light. More love. Stop hating things. Start loving everything."

That's *it*? Love is all you need?

The Beatles preached that fifty years ago. So has every religious type with long hair and a beard across millennia.

But maybe that's the point. The answers we keep searching for have been here all along. Love. Joy. *Everything is already inside, ready to roll.* Can getting on the magic bus be as simple as a smile that starts in your heart?

I've been aboard the painfully slow bus, where the path to love, joy and purpose is potholed with uncertainty and doubt. Failed relationships. Soul-crushing jobs. Feeling lost and directionless. I keep hoping for an epiphany to strike while I'm high on cacao, or stretching in a yoga class, or meditating on a mountain, that will connect all the dots and point to my life's purpose with a giant blinking arrow.

As I write this, I notice the mouse arrow on my screen and the blinking cursor next to my typed words. I smile, connecting my own dots. Getting out of my own way. At least long enough to publish something.

The Update

In the five years since I first met Keith and had the honor to attend the porch ceremonies described above, he has become one of my greatest teachers and his sweetheart Barbara has become a dear friend. I intentionally left intact my first impressions of Keith's cacao ceremonies, as they remain accurate and capture a particularly lost era of my life.

I have now learned a great deal more about cacao, and ceremonial cacao in particular. Enough to fill a whole separate book. There is no superfood more underestimated than cacao, and no term misunderstood more than cacao ceremony.

Keith draws undue criticism for being a white man "appropriating" a Mayan tradition, when in fact he uses no Mayan rituals or cultural elements in his ceremonies. Present-day indigenous shamans were not working exclusively with cacao when Keith made it his sole mission to make cacao more accessible to Westerners. He also began training a new generation of cacao practitioners in Guatemala and around the world. Trace any modern cacao ceremony leader (of any skin color) back a few teachers, and there's a good chance that one of them studied with Keith at some point. His unique ceremonies don't incorporate fire, special clothing or drums, as some indigenous ceremonies do. They simply harness the healing power of cacao as a medicine plant, the healing power of the Cacao Spirit consciousness beyond the plant, and the healing power already inside us all.

Keith gets visibly tearful when asked if cacao belongs solely to certain indigenous peoples. "What makes anyone think they can *own* a plant medicine? That someone can own the Cacao Spirit?" He recalls how he tried to learn about cacao from the local shamans when he first arrived in Guatemala twenty years ago, but none of them were really working with cacao. "I had to connect with the Cacao Spirit myself." She guided Keith to create a more potent, higher quality cacao that was ideal for inner work. Since then he has helped cacao spread across the globe, citing an ancient legend as his guiding mission: *When humanity falls out of harmony with the natural world, Cacao emerges from the rainforest to open people's hearts and restore the balance.* Recently a Mayan shaman told Keith that he is the first non-indigenous (white) person to truly understand cacao in 500 years.

Some who lack understanding are holding their own ceremonies and selling their own cacao to capitalize on its surging popularity. Keith doesn't mind the competition, but he is concerned about the poor quality and high caffeine content of many cacaos on the market today claiming to be ceremonial-grade. Unlike Keith's Cacao, they lack the active biochemical compounds needed to support real inner journeying, emotional processing, and healing work.

The products we all know more commonly as chocolate and cocoa powder have been largely stripped of the beneficial compounds that make pure, minimally processed cacao a uniquely powerful superfood: theobromine, anandamide, phenylethylamine (PEA), cacao butter, and oodles of antioxidants. Even much of the "100% pure cacao" sold today has been stripped of its potency through farming and production processes that favor profits and automation over retaining the healing properties that made ancient civilizations regard cacao as a divine medicine.

Keith's Cacao is sourced from the purest, rarest, non-hybridized Criollo variety of cacao—the hardest to grow and increasingly harder to find, accounting for just 1-5% of global cacao production. For many years Keith has employed dozens of local families in Guatemala with good wages and flexible working conditions, allowing many women to work from home while raising their children. He also helps finance emergency medical care and sponsors the local women's soccer team, the Pumas. The workers appear to regard Keith as family, and vice versa.

I knew none of this when I first stumbled onto Keith's porch back in 2018 for my very first cacao ceremony and first sip of real cacao. I could not imagine all the ways that experience would redirect my life in the years to come. The dear friends and future life partner I would meet on the porch, the personal and spiritual growth I would have as I continued working with Keith, the education on cacao that would inspire me to develop and teach an intensive course about its history, biology, health benefits and more.

"Someone should really write a book about this man," I remember thinking with awe on the day I first met Keith. I never imagined that someone would be me, nor that Keith would become inextricably linked to my own life story, my own purpose.

For those who are ready to get out of their own way, there is unimaginable love, meaning and magic brewing in a cup of cacao.

PART III: FINDING COURAGE

As a child I was scared a lot. Scared of darkness, strangers, speaking up in class. As an adult I became less shy, but fear still kept me from doing many things. "Fear, the worst of all enemies," Napoleon Hill advised, "can be effectively cured by forced repetition of acts of courage." So I repeatedly ran into the ocean to scuba dive, repeatedly taught yoga classes, and traveled alone for months at a time. These activities initially scared me. Then they changed my life. The following stories are about the wonders that await you on the other side of fear.

10

JOINING THE CULT OF SCUBA DIVING

Why divers are obsessed with diving, from a recent convert

"In Roatán, you either drink or you dive."

My friendly new neighbor, Rino, imparted this binary activity guide for how one generally allocates his time on a Honduran island that resembles a stock photo of a tropical paradise.

Rino owns a local dive shop, and his family is one of the oldest on the island, dating back centuries—to the pirate days—so if anyone can sum up life on Roa, it's probably him. But I had gathered enough conflicting evidence in my first week to flag a discrepancy.

"Actually, I've met quite a few people who seem to do plenty of both," I countered, citing recent evenings spent drinking with assorted divers, dive masters and instructors. With the world's second largest barrier reef in wading distance from the lively beachfront bars of Roatán's West End, some recreational crossover seemed inevitable.

LOST & FOUND

"You've got a point there," said Rino, laughing. We agreed that the diving-drinking combination was only concerning if done concurrently. Swim with the fish or drink like one. Never both.

As of that cloudy Caribbean day, I had only ever done the latter. But one week later, I completed my PADI open water dive training, with four official dives under my (eight-pound weight) belt.

I had spent the previous years traveling to premier diving destinations like Thailand, Belize and Bali and NOT diving—insisting to myself and anyone within earshot that snorkeling was satisfying enough. Diving simply seemed too high-maintenance to qualify as recreation.

Then I went from diving skeptic to addict overnight. The only people who weren't surprised? Divers. One of the annoying aspects of the diving cult I had actively resisted for so long was how fervently enamored its members were with diving. (Not to mention the arrogant tone they would use to correct you if you referred to fins as flippers.)

As someone on the outside, confined to floating on the surface like a dead fish, I continually rationalized that snorkeling had to be at least 80% as fulfilling as diving, with 0% of the bulky gear, latent arrogance and added risk of, you know, dying.

Perhaps I had listened to Jerry Seinfeld's stand-up bit on scuba diving one too many times. "Another great activity where your main goal is to *not die*. That's really all I thought about that day: [He sings] *Don't diieee, don't die don't die don't die—there's a fish, there's a rock—who cares? Don't die! I don't wanna die..."*

For reasons not entirely clear but at least partially rooted in procrastinating on the book I aspired to write, I decided it was finally time to learn how to die. I mean, dive. Plus, it seemed prudent to give my liver a break by re-allocating some of the time spent in dive bars toward actual dives.

Here is what no one tells you about diving while they're busy raving about how awesome it is: starting out suuucks. Those of us who didn't grow up in the water like Flipper or Michael Phelps feel like a silly, scared human whose elaborate attempt to pass for a fish isn't fooling anyone, not least of all our handsome French diving instructor.

"Alla, I'll be honest. That first day of your training in confined water, it seemed like maybe diving was not for you," Guillaume would later confess.

Okay, I'll admit I was terrified and one more involuntary gulp of seawater away from giving up. In my defense, that first day had involved practicing underwater skills like clearing a mask that's full of water (after flooding it with water on purpose) and retrieving your regulator, aka the breathing tube needed for survival (after losing it on purpose). Clearly handy techniques to master if you're going to be stationed sixty feet below sea level. But I had only just mastered the idea of being submerged on purpose and was even starting to believe on a primal level that I wasn't going to drown. After a very brief moment of relative comfort, it was time to simulate everything that could possibly go wrong.

LOST & FOUND

It would be like showing up on your first day of astronaut training, donning the full suit, and being tethered right into space. *Alright, Space Cowgirl, don't get too comfy. We're gonna start with all the crazy shit that could kill you. Go ahead and remove your helmet. That's right, just chuck it behind you, then simply retrieve it without panicking. I shall kindly demonstrate first, of course.*

In the midst of playing out emergency scenarios, you are also learning:

1. How to communicate through a slew of new hand signals (a thumbs-up is the *opposite* of 'I'm okay'—it means you want to go up to the surface)

2. How to control your body's buoyancy so you don't get sucked back up to the surface nor sink down to touch the fragile sea life on the ocean floor

3. How to use all the doodads on your aquatic jetpack (and how NOT to use them, like accidentally pressing the 'inflate' button on your BCD vest, which would be like auto-ejecting yourself out of a perfectly good submarine)

It's a master class in multi-tasking under pressure.

Guillaume was about the most patient, good-natured teacher a novice diver could have asked for, demonstrating each skill repeatedly with the comical expressiveness of a seasoned underwater mime. (That's fully intended as a compliment, not a jab at French performance artists). Every time I mastered a new skill, he double high-fived me underwater with the ecstatic pride of a parent whose kid just took her first steps. In her thirties.

After a rocky first day, my mastery thankfully accelerated. We moved from practicing in confined water (the nearby shallow bay) to open water (the actual endless ocean).

The bearable lightness of being a diver

The addition of depth in open water came with more skills to practice, and distractingly, more fish to look at. Emergency ascents, directional navigation, frequent equalizing of your air passages (to clear the clogged ears/nose feeling as you descend). And yet, I was shocked by how quickly I felt relaxed, even euphoric, amidst the expected anxieties of being the newest fish in the sea. The astronaut analogy bears reprisal, as they often train underwater, and while I haven't exactly been in space, gliding through the ocean's depths conjures parallels to what it might feel like Up There. Weightless. Free. Other-worldly.

Sometime during my first dive, it tipped from stressful to fun faster than you can say "anemone." Guillaume, sensing the shift in my energy, or perhaps noticing that the eyes inside my leak-prone mask no longer registered terror, stopped to scribble something on his waterproof notepad with a waterproof pencil: WELCOME :)

And that's exactly how I felt.

After four days in the water, scuba certification in hand, I fully intended to take a break from salty hair and pruney hands. But I awoke the next morning yearning to be seaborne. So I went snorkeling, but my low-maintenance old friend just wasn't the same. It was like going back to smoking weed after someone gave you a hit of heroin. Or so I'm told.

Why is diving such a high?

There are the obvious sensory enhancements. Seeing a beautiful, previously hidden layer of the world with your own eyes. Feeling weightless and free as you glide alongside a sea turtle that now regards you as an equal rather than a creeper gawking at it from above. Hearing the rhythmic sound of your own breath and the reassuring bubbles as you exhale.

Then there are the more subtle mental enhancements. Many divers report feelings of relaxation, a quieting of the mind, a deeper and more present meditative state without the usual distractions at the surface. After an hourlong dive, I would surface and find my mind to be completely silent on the boat ride back to shore. Diving had cut the mental chatter, putting me into a deep state of presence. I could simply take in the sights and sounds around me without getting sucked into my thoughts.

And then there is narcosis. Defined as a reversible alteration in consciousness that occurs while diving at depth, narcosis is caused by the anesthetic effect of certain gases at high pressure (in the case of recreational diving, the predominant gas in your tank is actually nitrogen, at 78%).

Narcosis produces a state similar to drunkenness or to nitrous oxide inhalation. The deeper you go, the more impairing its perception-altering symptoms. At my beginner descents within 60 feet, narcosis most commonly results in anxiety relief through feelings of tranquility, mild euphoria and mastery of one's environment.

Suddenly the link between drinking and diving takes on new meaning. As does the term *dive bar*. Narcosis is even nicknamed Rapture of the Deep and quantified by my new favorite maxim, Martini's Law.[8] People who wear lab coats estimate that for every 50 feet you descend underwater, breathing the compressed nitrogen from your tank has a similar effect on your brain as drinking one martini on an empty stomach.

Unlike with alcohol, the intoxicating effects of narcosis dissipate as soon as you ascend to shallower depths. Whether I went deep enough to experience very mild narcosis, or simply felt a beginner's buzz, is up for debate. Several weeks later I got my advanced certification and did a shipwreck deep dive at 110 feet on an empty stomach. I distinctly felt 'tipsy' for a moment, gripped with the sudden urge to giggle underwater for no particular reason.

It's worth noting that at depths below 140 feet, narcosis is no joke. It can severely impair your judgment to the point of death. I am making light of it at much shallower depths, where the symptoms are considerably more benign, if even noticeable.

I asked a dozen longtime divers from all over the world about Martini's Law, and regrettably no one had heard of it. All readily used terms like "addictive" and "it's a drug/high" to describe their relationship with diving, minus any destructive implications. The general consensus is that diving is good, clean, albeit pricey, fun—and not risky if you take the right precautions.

LOST & FOUND

As a new diver, am I predominantly high on mastery, high on sea turtle interaction, or high on nitrogen? Perhaps all of the above. Does it really matter? I suspect not. The things we love most in life often defy clear articulation as to why. Words are inadequate, not to mention useless, under the sea.

So despite the prevalence of inviting ocean-view bars and delicious daiquiris around the island, I can't wait to update Rino on my recreational preference: In Roatán, I only drink like a fish if I can't be near the little buggers.

※

Not only did I conquer my fear of diving, but it became an unexpected passion bordering on obsession. It was the hobby equivalent of a mistaken first impression, like meeting a person you initially hate who goes on to become your best friend. If you are drawn to something new but find yourself held back by fear or discomfort, perhaps allow my story to gently nudge you to "dive in" despite the fear. Most experiences get unimaginably better and easier with repetition—a future state we simply can't grasp from the sidelines.

After I left Roatán, I went on to dive with sharks and shipwrecks in the Philippines, car-sized manta rays in Indonesia's Komodo National Park, sunken statues in Bali, coral graveyards in Sri Lanka, and the vibrant reefs and sleepy turtles of Cozumel. I even became an amateur marine archaeologist during my bittersweet summer stay in Venice Beach—after I got dumped by Mister Synchronicity from Chapter 2, I became intimately acquainted with the surreal sport of megalodon shark tooth hunting (legally permitted in this part of Florida). These formidable giants went extinct over 3 million years ago, leaving their fossilized mega-teeth buried on the ocean floor. I went diving for "megs" every week, finding teeth between 3 and 4 inches long, envying the hand-sized 6-inch scores of my new dive buddies.

Within three years of my very first dive, I had racked up about seventy-five more across three continents. And that's when my diving passion and fearlessness became entangled in a net of foolish arrogance. The universe decided it was time I ate (and nearly choked on) a piece of humble pie, and so the next chapter was born.

Rino Jackson tragically passed away a few years after the encounters in this chapter occurred. I want to send love and gratitude to the memory of this legendary man, whose immense love of the sea was matched by a love for his fellow humans and beautiful homeland.

11

NEARLY DYING WHILE SCUBA DIVING

What a dear-death experience taught me about living

The Pit, or El Pit, as it's called here in Mexico, is one of the deepest cenotes (underwater caves) in the world. The main entrance is nature's grand ballroom. One hundred twenty feet deep and wide enough to fit a jumbo jet.

On sunny days the light rays pierce the clear blue water all the way down to the bottom. The effect makes you feel like you are in a dream. Today is such a day. El Pit is showing off.

The first half of my dive feels progressively more dreamlike the deeper we descend, in part due to chemistry. Our diving trio quickly discovers the cenote's halocene layer around 45 feet (15 meters). At this depth the freshwater from above mixes with the saltwater from below, creating a blurry effect as the light beams react to the different salinities.

Before the dive, our divemaster had briefed us about this unique phenomenon so we would not mistake the blurred view for a smudge on our mask lens. I know that my mask is clear, but my eyes are convinced we are floating in odorless oil.

Below the halocene layer, sharp clarity returns until we descend to 90 feet. Here lies an eerie cloud of hydrogen sulfide. It's like someone turned on a fog machine near the bottom of the cavern floor. As we swim closer, a bed of large rocks and naked tree branches beckon through the fog. The effect is both gloomy and gorgeous.

I gaze up at our small entry point a hundred feet above, where the sun pokes in and shines its laser beams all the way down to this Mayan underworld. Could this dive possibly get any better, I wonder. Could my life?

Overwhelmed by a sense of peace and calm as I often am while diving, I follow the divemaster deeper into the cenote, into a narrow chamber where we must rely entirely on our flashlights.

My mind is still calm, but I notice my heart rate accelerating. Perhaps I'm reacting to the cold and the dark? With the flashy attractions of the main cavern behind us, my awareness turns to unpleasantries.

My heart begins to race as if I were running at a sprint. But my body is barely moving. It doesn't make sense. How can my mind be thinking "I love this relaxing dive" while my heart thinks I'm out jogging with Usain Bolt? I will never make sense of what happens next.

I begin to hyperventilate. I can't catch my breath. This has never happened to me before in my life. Not on 75 previous dives, some involving sharks and shipwrecks and darkness.

LOST & FOUND

Not in decades of being physically active and mentally anxious.

I have heard of panic attacks described this way, like you can't breathe. But on dry land, even if you pass out, you will likely survive. I seem to have chosen the world's worst place and time to panic: while breathing a limited amount of oxygen through a regulator tube in my mouth—and during the deepest part of the dive, over 100 feet underwater. Ascending fast would give me serious decompression sickness, if not kill me.

So escaping to the surface is not an immediate option. This thought alone makes me panic more. I am stuck here. Try to calm down, I tell myself. In the history of mankind, have the instructions "calm down" ever worked on anyone?

The hyperventilating intensifies. My lungs feel like they're not getting enough air. Or getting too much air? Oh no. Nausea. I feel like I'm about to throw up. If I do, there's a chance I could drown in my own vomit inside the regulator. Another realization that does little to calm me down. (I will later remember that there *is* a way to clear vomit from a regulator, but the future is of no use to me right now.)

I use my flashlight to get the divemaster's attention, shining the hand signal that means *Something is wrong*. I am enveloped in air bubbles from my erratic exhales. He swims over and grabs my hand, attempting to calm me and stabilize my buoyancy.

It does nothing to calm me, however. I am still gasping for air, still fighting the urge to vomit. I feel alone and scared, and the whisper that says I'm going to die grows louder.

ALLA POLSKY

A crushing wave of sadness washes over me. Could this really be how it ends? What a lame and lonely way to die, far away from everyone I love, deep underground in this cold, dark, wet cave. For seemingly no reason, while doing something I love, or at least have loved up until this terrifying moment.

A stream of unhelpful thoughts all meld together: *If I die, there will be two funerals—my mother won't survive this. Herb will say "See, I told you! Diving IS dangerous." No, I am not ready. There's still so much I want to do in this life. But this moment hurts too much. If I AM going to die, can we speed through the drowning part? I'm ready.*

I am completely oblivious to the surroundings outside my malfunctioning mind and body. Oblivious to the feel of another diver's hand holding mine.

Suddenly I notice that we have drifted toward a vertical wall of limestone. Instinctively I touch it with my free hand, yearning for something solid and steadfast to hold on to.

Something shifts. My heart rate instantly begins to settle. I let go of the divemaster's hand so I can place both of my palms on the wall. My heart rate returns to normal within seconds.

Holy hell. All I needed was a little *grounding*?

I feel emotionally shaken, but my body has returned to a peaceful resting state, like nothing even remotely life-threatening just happened. Like there was no fight or flight—only float. *Did* something happen, or is this old, mystical cave simply messing with me?

My instinct tells me to continue on with the dive. That surfacing now would symbolize a newfound fear of diving, a fear I do not want. So I give the *I'm okay* hand signal to my divemaster, genuinely feeling okay in that moment. Feeling more than okay, because I am still alive, suddenly grateful for the ease of each breath. We dive on.

The next twenty minutes are relatively uneventful. We gradually ascend to shallower depths, view stalactite formations, do a safety stop at 15 feet, and return to the surface. Still wearing our heavy gear, we climb the wooden ladder out of the cenote, the same way we came in.

Except I do not feel like the same person who came in. Something has shifted.

I will never know how close I actually came to death. (I will later learn that over 20% of diving deaths are directly caused by panic attacks, and that 1 in 4 divers has experienced at least one.) Trapped in that particular moment, I fully believed I was close to death. I was nearly certain. I saw no way out. And I was ready to die if it meant putting an end to the physical pain and to the sad, lonely thoughts that would be my very last thoughts.

I believe a part of me did die in that cave. The part that was holding me back my whole life. The scared, insecure part that kept me small and safe. Kept my heart cautiously closed.

The shift was nearly imperceptible at first. But since that dive, I have been living more openly. I have finally stopped stalling on the things I am meant to do, even if they scare me. Like teaching yoga classes. Like falling in love for the first time in ten years. And writing about all of it.

Enough stalling, I figure. I didn't maybe almost die so I could maybe almost live. It's time to live.

Is the valuable lesson here to minimize contact with cold, dark, underwater caves, or to not let courage turn into foolish overconfidence? Perhaps a bit of both. I think this can be applied far beyond diving. Challenges will inevitably arise long after you have mastered a skill or conquered a fear. They help prevent us from becoming arrogant and careless, while reminding us that there is always more to learn.

Challenges may bring stress, but they also bring gifts. The terrifying experience of believing I was moments away from death left me with a deeper courage and gratitude for my life than I could previously imagine. A deep sea panic attack was certainly not high on my adventure bucket list, but it did reboot my nervous system in a way that wouldn't be possible on dry land. A way that continues to center me, teach me, and humble me long after I found my way back to the surface.

12

NEARLY READY TO TEACH YOGA

And why there's no such thing as ready

On the day I signed up for a 15-day, 200-hour yoga teacher training in Costa Rica, I awoke that morning with absolutely no clue that I was about to alter the course of my life.

As my once exciting days in Manhattan had morphed into mostly exhausting, yoga was one of the few things that kept me sane. I was attending group classes once or twice a week and doing a brief morning practice daily at home. Teaching yoga had never crossed my mind.

A few days earlier my mind had decided it was time to leave New York. My heart was no longer in it. Six years was enough. I had given notice to my boss and my landlord. In a few weeks I would have to vacate my apartment. I had no idea where I was going, geographically or existentially.

Travel was calling me, the lifestyle for lost souls, but where to go? I had backpacked around Southeast Asia a few years back and loved it. Perhaps I could explore South America this time, stay a little closer to home. At that moment I felt paralyzed by too much choice, not ready to plan much of anything.

Oh, I've got it! I shall ease into my travels on a note of clarity and relaxation. I Googled "yoga retreats in Costa Rica." And that's when the search algorithm gods serendipitously served up the words that would change my life: yoga teacher training.

An upcoming one in Costa Rica immediately caught my eye. It took an hour of research and reading to convince my rational mind of what I already knew in my heart: I had to do this training. Plus, I rationalized further, most one-week yoga retreats seemed to cost about as much as an entire teacher training. Did I simply want to be pampered and stretch my body for a week, or stretch my mind for a lifetime?

Particularly among women, it has become increasingly common to obtain a yoga teacher certification after years of dissatisfaction working in a very different field. The cliché was captured in a made-up report in *The Onion*, the internet's satirical news source. "According to a Department of Labor report on job retraining, 21% of American women are training to be yoga instructors."

On that cloudy fall day in New York, I would join not only this fictional 21%, but as I would later learn, the real uncertain majority who would sign up for a rigorous teacher training without any conscious intent to teach.

While I loved the idea of deepening my own practice and understanding the philosophy behind it, would I really feel ready after 200 hours of training to start sharing that practice and understanding with others? Would I even *want* to?

LOST & FOUND

Before I could answer those questions, I would first need to survive the 15-day spiritual bootcamp in the jungle that characterizes the most accelerated yoga teacher training on the market. While most trainings spread out the required 200 hours of instruction across three to four weeks or even months, the one that had caught my eye offered a shorter, more intensive two-week immersion.

The course would be led by Marianne Wells, a lifelong yoga teacher and founder of Costa Rica's longest running yoga teacher training. I had a brief phone call with Marianne to address any questions or concerns either of us might have about spending fifteen long days together to eat, sleep, and breathe nothing but yoga.

My impulsive urge to join her next training in a few weeks didn't seem to scare her. She assured me it was quite common to enroll last-minute yogis and only asked that I approach the experience with an open mind and open heart—and do the work.

I needed that open mind a few hours later when I received the training preparation instructions via email. The packing list included the following disclaimer: "Please bring your own bath towel and bed linens if you have brightly colored hair that bleeds when wet."

What? How many of my fellow aspiring teachers have brightly colored hair? It must be a sizable percentage to make it into the official packing instructions. I wondered what hue would be the most popular this year. Organic orange? Blissful blue? Heart chakra green?

ALLA POLSKY

I wasn't actually worried that the training would be full of strange hippies who would weird me out. I was more worried that *I* wouldn't fit *in*, with my boring naturally colored hair and my corporate career history.

Neither scenario materialized. My training group was a delightful motley crew from all over the world and all kinds of backgrounds. Our ages ranged from 18 to 65. Out of 44 people, five were men—a decent turnout in such a female-dominated space. "Broga," I remembered reading somewhere with amusement, is going to be the next big fitness craze, making yoga more accessible to men.

Some of the yogis in my training class were starting their very first career. Others were ready to leave behind many years in law or finance. A comforting majority were like me—not yet sure if they wanted to teach yoga as their main job, or a side gig, or ever teach at all.

On the first full day of training, I did not feel fully ready for the 6 a.m. morning practice, nor for meeting 43 new souls who could all presumably balance on their pinkies upside down while reading the Yoga Sutras with their third eye.

As I got to know them over the next few weeks, my imposter syndrome subsided. I realized they were regular people just like me who all overcame their own fears and insecurities to be here. Most of them were not yoga gymnasts or contortionists. Hell, no one even had blue hair. Their lives and backgrounds may have looked different from mine on paper, but beneath the facts, a deeper universal truth emerged. On some level we were all here in search of major change and transformation—in both our professional and personal lives.

LOST & FOUND

We were all bound by this search, by our readiness for change. Some of our paths would stay entwined for years to come.

My roommate in the training would become one of my dearest friends. Mia was a U.S. Marine Corps lieutenant and a former competitive body-builder. She could pick me up and bench press me—and did, on several amusing occasions. Mia came to the teacher training at a major crossroads in her life. Should she stay in the Marines, taking on bigger leadership roles and more responsibility? Or leave the military for good, shedding an identity that had defined her entire adult life, not to mention the lives of her brothers, sister, and father?

On the surface Mia's job description could not have appeared more different from mine. I sat safely in an office building, occasionally making PowerPoint presentations for meetings. Mia occasionally jumped out of airplanes in countries I am probably not supposed to name. But both of us found our jobs to be unfulfilling in the same way: they were stressful, tiring, and lacked a spiritual component that had become increasingly important in our lives.

Shortly after our teacher training, Mia decided to remain in the Marines. She was chosen for a highly selective leadership program, which felt like a sign to stay. But a few years later, she finally left for good and enrolled in a graduate school to study Chinese medicine. Healing people has always been her calling. It's what drew her to a yoga teacher training, even if she didn't fully know it yet.

We had a saying at the training: *the days are long, but the weeks are short.* Every morning we awoke before 5 a.m. to the sound of howler monkeys, the rainforest's unavoidable alarm clock. Each day was packed from head to barefoot toes with yoga practice, anatomy lectures, philosophy discussions, class sequencing, adjustments, Ayurveda, chakras, mantras, and nightly homework. Lights out by 11 p.m. to bend, breathe, and repeat all over again. Yet somehow those interminably long 15 days flew by in a single flash.

Having survived the spiritual bootcamp, I was now confronted with the tougher part: figuring out if I actually wanted to be a yoga teacher. More pointedly, if I *didn't* want to teach, was it because my heart wasn't called to it or because I was simply scared to suck at something (an inevitable reality of starting out)?

In the months after the training, I watched from the sidelines as my fellow graduates began to teach. Even Mia was teaching yoga at her local gym. Hearing their tales of first-class-butterflies, forgotten sequences and ultimately "It wasn't as hard as I thought!" filled me with vicarious joy and a tinge of envy.

Deep down I knew I was being a coward. I really did want to try my hand at teaching. But whenever the opportunity arose, even in a casual setting among friends, I declined. My brain was scared to fail, to be bad at something, or be anything less than perfect. It was a pattern that had plagued me since childhood, causing me to abandon any pursuit I couldn't master with relative ease—learning to play the guitar, for instance.

LOST & FOUND

Fortunately the universe wasn't ready to abandon *me* on this yoga thing yet. Exactly one year after my teacher training, Marianne invited me to return to Costa Rica as a teaching assistant. I got a thorough review of all the training material, plus the priceless experience of helping other aspiring teachers complete their training. I watched with pride as many of them went on to teach. Once again I remained on the sidelines, stuck in a disappointing Groundhog's Day loop.

It would take six years from the moment I completed my training to the moment I finally taught my first class. The offer I couldn't refuse came from Herb and our hostel. We were holding yoga classes for our guests several days a week, and one of our regular teachers suddenly had to leave town for a month. We had no one to take her place on short notice. This was my chance.

I wanted to be helpful to Herb, our hostel, and our guests. Finally the part of me that longed to teach overruled the part of me that was scared and not ready.

I over-prepared, talked too much, then didn't talk enough. Teaching my first class to a packed room with Herb in the front row, I felt awkward, nervous, and amateurish. But I did it. And I grew noticeably more comfortable with each subsequent class. There were no major screw-ups, aside from the mishap described later in Chapter 17. Similar to my experience with diving, teaching yoga tipped from stressful to fun faster than you can say *asana*.

An Irish backpacker who had taken my very first class returned to the hostel a few months later. He marveled at how much my classes had improved in such a short time. "You were a good teacher from the start, but now you are so natural and so fully enjoying it. Today was one of my favorite yoga classes ever!"

He wasn't just saying it to be nice. I could feel it, too.

While I was busy worrying about sucking as a teacher, I forgot that it's not actually about *me*. It's about *them*. All the people I could be serving. Helping them fall in love with yoga like I had. Guiding them through a practice that quiets their mind, strengthens their body, and connects them more deeply with their inner spirit.

Now I can't help but wonder how many phenomenal new teachers are out there today, whether in yoga or something else, just sitting on the fence waiting until they are "ready". Being the cowardly lion like I was. There will never be a perfect time to start something new, and never a shortage of legitimate sounding excuses for why it can't be now.

The universe is always ready for you to do what you were meant to do. But it will wait patiently for you to run out of excuses, like it did with me for six years.

> *It's a terrible thing, I think, in life to wait until you're ready. I have this feeling now that actually no one is ever ready to do anything. There is almost no such thing as ready. There is only now. And you may as well do it now. Generally speaking, now is as good a time as any.* —Hugh Laurie, actor

LOST & FOUND

Jokes—and the lure of wearing yoga pants to work—aside, changing careers is scary. Starting over is scary. Doing something new for the first time, like teaching an hourlong class, can be socially terrifying. But what is more scary is never doing the things that could bring your soul home, and help countless other souls, because you didn't ever feel quite ready enough.

An ancient proverb mirrors Laurie's modern take on readiness:

> *The best time to plant a tree was twenty years ago. The second best time is now.*

Plant that first seed, take the first step, and life will fall into place—whether you're ready or not.

13

FULLY READY TO TRAVEL ALONE

Contrary to popular belief, solo travel is not a social desert

When I tell people that I have traveled solo for months at a time, I predictably hear a lot of "That's awesome!" and "I'm so jealous!" and "How the heck do you pay for that?"

(Long-term travel is delightfully affordable in most parts of the world, a topic detailed by countless travel writers and vloggers.)

A close friend confessed that another question often gets asked after I leave the room. Not out of mean-spirited gossip but a polite desire to spare my feelings.

"Doesn't she get lonely? I think I would start to feel lonely out there on her own."

I want to answer this question for anyone else wondering, and for my own sanity. Before I started traveling solo, this was my top concern beyond general safety. Would I have to eat every meal at a table-for-one while Celine Dion's "All By Myself" blared from a rusty jukebox? Would there be no one to watch sunsets with—and more upsettingly, no one to take silhouetted photos of me doing yoga during sunsets?

Luckily it didn't take long to dispel the myth of the Lone-Ness Monster.

Travel comes with different social norms

I quickly realized that I felt considerably less alone doing things by myself when I traveled than back at home. And it's not because thousands of miles away, I didn't have to worry about being spotted dining solo by someone I knew. (The fear of social judgment largely dissipated in my thirties, a pleasant side effect of aging that doctors refer to as "giving fewer f*ck s.") When you travel, there are entirely different social norms that make it hard to get lonely—unless, of course, you choose to actively repel people by being a jerk.

Travel actually reverses all the isolating social taboos of regular life, which is partly why I fell in love with the nomad lifestyle. Instead of *Don't talk to strangers*, it's *Definitely talk to strangers.* People are infinitely more chatty and approachable on the road, especially if they are on their own. Conversing with strangers is not only logistically essential but socially encouraged. Asking a simple question like, "Which way to the famous temple, or the nearest working ATM?" often results in a shared stroll, a shared meal, or even a lasting friendship.

Instead of *Act like you know where you're going* (on the street and in life), it's *Being lost is a given. Feel free to ask for directions and/or discuss your existential crisis about feeling directionless in life!* Chances are, these traveling strangers can relate. I once shared a taxi from Guatemala City airport to Antigua with a young British backpacker on his first solo trip. We sped through the formalities of *where are you from/been/going?* and went straight to existential crises. He confessed the main reason he decided to travel was because at home he felt lonely and lost while everyone else was having kids and careers. "But out here," he countered, "We're sort of supposed to be lost, aren't we?" I laughed and agreed wholeheartedly that being lost feels considerably less lame and reassuringly more common when you are in a foreign country on the other side of the world.

Back in New York City, it would have taken a few strong drinks at happy hour to get coworkers I have known for years to open up so candidly about their problems. But in a broad daylight Guatemalan taxi with a sober guy I have known for five minutes, the personal stuff pours out from both of us. That's because travel is an alternate reality with vastly different social rules. More specifically, there aren't any.

Have you ever sat next to a stranger on a long flight and bared your soul to them because you knew you would never see them again? Traveling solo is like that flight, except you don't even care if you see them again or not. You still bare your soul regardless, and so do they. In fact, it's highly probable that you *will* bump into them again at some point on the predictable travel trail. Before you know it, without even trying, you have made a new dear friend for life.

Strangers rarely remain so

In the proverbial "real world" it gets harder to make new friends with every trip around the sun. People get social tunnel vision, naturally gravitating toward hanging out with people they already know they like, or within the new families they are spawning with their spouse. But during travels, it's genuinely hard *not* to make new friends. Everyone is away from their tunnels, their childhood friends and their comfort zones. They, too, have decided to travel in part to expand their horizons and social spheres.

During my solo trips, genuine friendships formed fast and spontaneously, often in the span of a few days or one lengthy bus ride. Exchanging travel tips and life stories with virtual strangers came so naturally that I sometimes felt like I was cheating on my longtime friends back home.

When I chose to linger more than a few days in the same town, I no longer felt alone at all. I repeatedly ran into the same fellow travelers, which is probably not that surprising probability-wise, but it feels like needle-in-a-haystack-fate each time it happens. Like the universe is saying, "Of all the longitudes and latitudes in all the world, you guys keep converging here, so you might as well, like, hang out." (In my mind the universe apparently sounds like a surfer dude who watched *Casablanca*.)

Sure, we might run into people repeatedly back at home, perhaps on the daily train commute or at the gym. But we rarely appreciate the synchronicity in these seemingly more mundane run-ins. At most we'll say 'hey' and scurry back into our tunnels. Rarely do we cross the acquaintance line and invite them to a local ceramics market or drum circle like we would whilst traveling, thereby sparking the beginning of a beautiful friendship and a shared lakefront rental house with stunning views and a leaky roof (T, I'm looking at you).

Traveling solo is what singles do

Back in my single days—er, decade, I actually traveled in part to feel *less* lonely. Regular life is built around couples. When you are in a relationship, you rarely notice this, because your life follows the factory settings our society has preset. Most tables default to two-seaters, hotels default to double occupancy, and weddings default to inviting you and your plus-one.

If you are still a minus-one in your late thirties like I was, you can barely take a breath without being reminded that every inhale should be coupled with an exhale. For many singles, travel is a godsend. Yes, there are plenty of couples abroad. But increasingly there are many more single people traveling for extended periods of time. A good chunk are newly single—taking a big trip often occurs in the wake of a recent breakup.

For me traveling solo while single wasn't always easy or lonely-proof (see the next chapter), but on average it felt liberating and exciting. Romantic connections formed as fast as friendships, and though they could also fizzle fast, this was preferable to the drawn-out casual dating scene back home. Of course rejections and frustrations still happened, but it was unbelievably easy to meet nice, alluring, interesting people every day without the use of a single dating app.

In my single days I once wrote about a phenomenon called travel-hot, whereby men in travel mode appear considerably hotter than they would back home. You can blame their sun-kissed hiking tans, rugged facial hair, and sexy accessories like surfboards and guitars for fogging up your normally sensible romance radar. Assuming they shower with some regularity, most people just seem more attractive when they travel. Herb's own transformation into travel hotness included growing out his hair from spiky short to Jesus-length, losing a few pounds, gaining a short beard, and buying a motorcycle in Mexico. I didn't stand a chance.

Alone is paradoxically more social

Recently at our favorite coffee shop, Herb and I lamented the fact that you meet considerably fewer people when traveling as a couple. Without intending to, we create a little bubble that deters people from approaching us, except to borrow the occasional salt shaker from our table. Others unconsciously assume we may be talking about something private, or that we simply prefer to stay in our bubble. If we wish to make friends, *we* must be the ones to break the ice and initiate contact. Or we can simply split up on occasion.

Just yesterday I sat alone on the second floor of a restaurant, gazing at volcanoes and sipping cacao while waiting for Herb to join me for lunch. Suddenly the ground began to shake. "I think that's an earthquake," said the guy at the next table. "I think you're right," I replied. That ground shaker was an icebreaker. We ended up chatting for the next hour. What started as small talk about the Richter scale quickly segued into big talk about relationships, business goals, and healing journeys. I had fully intended to spend the time alone reading a book, but the universe felt I should make a new friend and sent an earthquake to break the ice. Herb showed up halfway into the conversation and joined right in. I was glad to have been alone long enough to spark the new connection for us both, before we burrowed into our dining bubble.

When alone is a choice, it rarely feels lonely

Another reason that travel feels refreshingly un-lonely has to do with choice and free will. There are plenty of scenarios in life where people feel lonely. Many of them happen right at home. Psychologists have proclaimed loneliness as the new epidemic threatening society, estimated to be more harmful to our health than smoking 15 cigarettes a day.

There is no shortage of legitimate reasons to feel lonely these days. We can blame the superficial nature of social media and online dating, the splintering of families across different cities, ever-lengthening work hours, and the added isolation of the pandemic.

For me the loneliest moments of my life boiled down to feeling like I didn't *choose* this solitude, when I had zero choice in the matter. Like on countless Saturday nights in New York, when I craved human connection and perhaps a nice dinner with my future husband, and instead I was left with Netflix and a bag of overpriced Terra chips (which, don't get me wrong, are delicious). Sure, I could have dragged another single friend to another bar, but that choice had already been made a hundred times and led to predictable disappointment.

When I decided to travel alone, however, I was back in the driver's seat of my life. I chose this momentary solitude, this freedom, this adventure. And none of it was ever the least bit predictable.

The least lonely I have ever felt in my life was the five days I chose not to talk to anyone on purpose. My silent meditation retreat in Guatemala was every bit as eye-opening as it was mouth-closing. I thought cutting myself off from human interaction might feel isolating, but it was actually quite liberating when the option (and pressure) to socialize was completely gone. Instead of feeling disconnected, I felt *more* connected to the oneness of all beings, to the wonders of nature, and to myself.

Alone is powerful, not pathetic

Western culture is obsessed with individualism, with carving one's own path, and yet paradoxically stigmatizes the lone individual. Growing up we are taught a very simple social dichotomy: You are cool if you go to parties and sporting events / You are a loser if you stay home with a book.

Yes, we are social animals who need human connection, but we mistakenly treat solitude as the enemy of happiness rather than a necessary aspect of personal growth.

Being alone is usually a punishment—and never, ever a reward. When kids misbehave, we send them on a time-out to their room or ground them from seeing their friends. When adults misbehave in the worst way possible, we isolate them in solitary confinement or exile them to a desolate faraway land forever.

As a society we shun the loners and the introverts. We conflate being lonely and being alone, as if loneliness magically disappears when we surround ourselves with other people. I have felt more lonely standing in the middle of a crowded party on New Year's Eve than I have while sitting on a quiet mountain top or lakeside dock at sunrise, without a single other soul in sight. After all, it's hard to feel lonely when you are busy being rendered speechless by the beauty of this world and the inter-connectedness of everything.

Whether you have the interest and opportunity to travel solo or not, the benefits can be felt much closer to home. See what happens if you simply go out for a solitary meal at a new restaurant in your hometown, or sit in a public park and people watch, the way you would in a foreign country. Don't look at your phone. Look around, look inward. In this moment, solitude is your choice, a little gift to yourself. You might realize, much to your surprise:

> *Solitude isn't Loneliness. Solitude is when the entire universe seems to surround and hold you quietly.* —Victoria Erickson

Does traveling alone get lonely? Sure, at times. So does traveling with other people, especially the wrong people. Life at home gets lonely, too, with and without others.

I was constantly surrounded by people when I lived in New York, yet I was often lonely. My friends loved me, but they couldn't relate to my increasingly itchy feet and restless soul. The city still felt like home to them. To me it felt like all those pairs of stylish yet torturous high heels I could no longer bear to walk in. So I left in search of more comfortable footwear and more fulfilling strolls. On a deeper level I was searching for that elusive thing most of us hope to find when we trade the familiar comforts of home for the complete unknown: Happiness.

PART IV: FINDING HAPPINESS

Here we go. The big H. Probably the most sought after, and most elusive, thing in the world. The more we chase after it, the farther away it seems to get. Finding happiness is completely entwined with finding the other goodies in this book. Love, purpose, courage, enlightenment. The stories in this section don't guarantee or over-promise. They simply speak from experience and strive to offer a fresh perspective on being happy.

14

CAN YOU ACTUALLY TRAVEL YOURSELF HAPPY?

For five years I chased happiness around the world. The answer surprised me.

Here is the plot of most movies and books involving travel: Person's life sucks. Person takes a long trip to somewhere exotic. Life improves greatly. Person writes a bestseller about the adventure, it gets made into a movie, and the travel-yourself-happy plan captivates those of us still stuck in Act One of the plot.

This life improvement strategy was likely simmering in my subconscious when my landlord shoved a lease renewal form under the door of my tiny studio apartment in New York City.

I had felt vaguely unhappy and directionless for years, lying to everyone including myself every time I went jogging in my I ♥ NY t-shirt. I didn't completely hate my life, nor the city I had called home for the last six years. There was simply a growing void of loneliness I could no longer fill with late nights at the office or weekend drinks with friends.

I had no idea where to go next. I just knew I couldn't sign that lease for another year.

LOST & FOUND

More than five years would pass until I had a somewhat permanent address again: the hostel with Herb in Chiapas, Mexico (then eventually Lake Atitlán, Guatemala). The winding journey in between gave me temporary homes in 22 countries on four different continents.

I was unimaginably happy in every single one.
HA, JUST KIDDING!
I cried on several continents. I had heartbreaks and breakdowns. I felt lost. I felt alone. I *was* alone. I spent holidays without loved ones. Birthdays with complete strangers. I nearly convinced myself I would be alone forever. Nearly gave up hope that I'd ever be truly happy anywhere.

It took me about a dozen passport stamps to realize something: I didn't want to be somewhere else. I wanted to be SOMEONE else.

I was using travel as a beautiful band-aid for a lifelong wound: I had never really liked myself. Always fixating on my flaws and insecurities instead of my gifts and strengths. All the gorgeous Greek islands in the world couldn't make me happy if I felt ugliness inside.

> *How can you wonder your travels do you no good, when you carry yourself around with you?*
> —Socrates

Thanks, Socrates. This question would have been super useful five years earlier. I had to figure it out the hard way.

ALLA POLSKY

As it turns out, if you are not fundamentally happy on the inside, relocating to exotic locales might cheer you up momentarily, but never for long. That nagging sense of loneliness and aimlessness I felt while living in New York? It followed me around the world. It spoiled surf lessons in Bali, rooftop dinners in Morocco, and sunrise hikes in Sri Lanka.

It wasn't all bad, of course. I felt daily gratitude for my nomadic freedom. I was constantly humbled by the beauty of the world and the kindness of strangers. I made true friends and had the kinds of adventures you could write a book about. But still I felt a void. Something missing. Exploring a new country didn't fill the void for long. Because I didn't want to be somewhere else—I wanted to be someone else. Someone prettier or more confident or more certain of her life purpose.

One year around Christmas, Santa would have found me sobbing on the shore of a Philippine island, my tears merging with the saltiness of the sea. I was traveling with a good friend at the time, but that didn't stop my old friend Sadness from whispering cold thoughts on a warm, moonlit night. *If you can't even be happy here in paradise, you will never be happy Anywhere.*

I reached a breaking point that night, and a breakthrough that didn't bring much comfort at the time. I was literally living in paradise. Staying in a cozy beachfront cabin for about $15 (USD) a night, including breakfast. Diving with majestic thresher sharks, their enlarged eyes and elongated tails like a Pixar creature. One of my dearest friends was with me. I was not alone. The local islanders were incredibly kind. The weather was perfect. And yet despite all of these blessings, I felt a deep sadness.

The breakthrough: with nothing external to blame my sadness on, I knew without a teary doubt that it was coming from inside. From my own repressed, unprocessed issues. It had been considerably easier to blame my sadness on external factors back in New York (a stressful job, dreary winters, high rent, tough dating scene). But here in perfect paradise, the only problem was me.

That island night, I finally confronted my demons and began to take responsibility for them. It was no one else's fault that I felt lonely, that I dwelled on my insecurities, that I pushed love away because I was scared to feel it again. I didn't quite know how to conquer these demons, but at least I was done pretending they didn't exist. And I was done hoping that island hopping to the next beautiful place would magically make them disappear.

You can't get away from yourself by moving from one place to another. —Ernest Hemingway

One thing is certain: Hemingway and Socrates would have made ideal travel companions.

Can you truly travel yourself happy?

Here's the thing. Despite what Hollywood suggests, travel is not a silver bullet toward happiness and fulfillment. Your emotional baggage will always sneak itself into your luggage.

And you will likely experience some loneliness, lostness, and mosquito bites.

BUT—there's a massive upside. Travel pushes you out of your comfort zone. And if you let it, it accelerates your personal growth. Travel allows you to engineer a lifestyle that is more conducive to dealing with and healing your inner demons than the lifestyle that created them.

> *We cannot solve our problems with the same thinking we used when we created them.* —Albert Einstein

Can you travel yourself happy? Yes, if you are willing to use the time to work on yourself, rather than simply distract yourself with beautiful scenery or nonstop partying. Yes, if you are honest with yourself about how you need to grow and evolve. Yes, if you are willing to love yourself more, not less, no matter how long it takes to become that person.

As I started to realize this, my travels changed from speeding through tourist attractions to slowing down and tuning in to my true passions. I began to balance paid freelance work with personal inner work. I made more meaningful connections with others.

I went to meditation classes, cacao ceremonies, and yoga trainings. I learned to scuba dive, to surf, to play the ukulele, to enjoy my own company. I published writing, made lifelong friends, shed insecurities. I truly began to love the person I was becoming—and more importantly, the person I already was.

I had no idea that any of this would happen when I decided not to renew my New York apartment lease. I simply knew I couldn't stay.

For years I chased happiness around the world. Until I realized I was like a dog chasing my own tail. It's trite but true. The only place we ever feel happiness is inside ourselves. We might think that happiness was caused by an external event or another person, but that's simply a story our mind attached to the happy feeling. The same goes for unhappiness. It is easy and tempting to blame it on others. People hurting you, life letting you down. But strip away all those external triggers, like I finally did in an island paradise, and you realize that your unhappiness is coming from deep within. This may sound like a downer, but it's also kind of empowering. If our own traumas and insecurities are the main source of our unhappiness, then the power to heal them also lies within.

Travel is not a guaranteed ticket toward a happier, more fulfilling life. But it can accelerate the process if you allow it. It can help excavate the version of you that was there all along, buried under an avalanche of societal expectations, academic pressures, self-doubts and whatever else steered you off course from following your inner compass toward joy.

Can you find your way there without travel? Of course. It's just infinitely more fun out there.

The over-pursuit of happiness

ALLA POLSKY

When I realized I could use travel to accelerate my personal growth and happiness, I may have gone a bit overboard. I started with a yoga teacher training in Costa Rica, followed immediately by hiking the Inca Trail in Peru. Being surrounded by the ancient Inca energy and the beauty of nature, it was easy to feel happier and more connected.

I got addicted to that feeling and started chasing *it* around the world, forgetting that it was inside me, not out there. I was unconsciously searching for some magical shortcut to lasting happiness. I was high on travel, and spiritual travel in particular, bouncing from Tibetan yoga classes in Nepal to Buddhist temples in Sri Lanka to Mayan sweat lodges and meditation centers in Guatemala. No matter the country, I began to gravitate toward more 'spiritual' activities over general sightseeing.

And I wasn't alone. There is a large global community of soul-seekers, flocking to the same spiritual hotspots around the world. Sedona, Arizona and Taos, New Mexico in the U.S. Ubud in Bali. Goa in India. Tulum in Mexico. Lake Atitlán in Guatemala. Some of these spots have arguably been "ruined" by their reputation, becoming overrun with people, straining the local resources, driving up prices, and drowning out the peaceful vibe that made them popular in the first place.

I ran into the same exact backpackers in Southeast Asia as I did on the other side of the world in Central America. *The world is SO small,* I marveled. It isn't, though. The world remains massive. The spiritual tourism world, however, feels increasingly tiny and well-trodden. This isn't inherently a bad thing (over-tourism aside). Nor is there anything inherently wrong with seeking self-improvement, deeper happiness, and higher states of consciousness.

Only you know deep down if you are packing your schedule full of healing sound baths and plant medicine ceremonies because you are ready to do your inner work and face your shadows, or because you are actually avoiding sitting still with them. In the therapy world this is called therapy jumping. Hopping from one therapeutic technique or healing modality to another, not sticking with anything long enough to see real progress. Your conscious mind might believe you are seeking out help, but on a subconscious level you don't actually want to feel better yet.

It's the same with travel jumping. I didn't consciously realize that I was hopping around the globe in search of spiritual highs—from crystals workshops to chakra realignments to kundalini awakenings—until the pandemic made me stop hopping altogether. I finally saw that most of these spiritual pursuits had done little to cleanse my aura of its underlying issues. The sadness and loneliness were still there.

When I stopped looking for the magic fix *out there*, I started tuning in to my own inner magic. As cheesy as that sounds, it worked. I surrendered to the reality of being stuck in Texas indefinitely with my family after years of exploring the globe. To my own surprise, I found peace and contentment in being nowhere. In being back where I started. I unearthed genuine joy in the simplest acts: playing my old piano to the backdrop of a summer thunderstorm, going on daily walks with my mom through the suburbs, listening to my grandmother's wartime stories and even to the reassuring sound of her snoring during daytime naps.

When I began traveling again as the world slowly opened up, I had opened up, too. I no longer expected travel to magically solve my problems. I knew I could solve them myself, in beautifully simple ways that are a kind of everyday magic.

Long-term travelers are often unconsciously looking for happiness in that next destination. With so much freedom and mobility, it's tempting to think, If I'm not 100% loving it *here*, perhaps I'll be happier in the *next* place I visit. Though I had started traveling in pursuit of happiness, I found considerably more value in slowing down and standing still long enough to face the parts of myself I had been trying to get away from all along.

Whether your passport pages are regrettably empty or impressively full, this is a courtesy reminder that no amount of entry stamps will fulfill you like facing your emotional baggage, inner demons, and the real reason you are traveling in the first place.

15

NOT GETTING YOUR WAY IS A GIFT FROM THE FUTURE

A modern spin on the old proverb 'Good Luck, Bad Luck'

You may have heard a version of this ancient proverb about the wise old farmer and his horse.

An old farmer had a single horse. It helped plow the field, sow the seeds, and transport the crops to the market. That horse was his livelihood. One day the horse ran away. His neighbors came over to express condolences. "What rotten luck! How will you provide for your family now?"

The old man was unfazed. "Good luck, bad luck. Who knows? It is what it is. My horse is gone."

A few days later, the horse returned—with a herd of wild horses. This time the villagers came to offer their congratulations at such a stroke of good luck. More horses meant more income! "What a godsend," they said.

"Good luck, bad luck. Who knows?" replied the old man again. "All I see is that more horses have appeared."

The next week, while breaking in one of the wild horses, the old man's son fell and broke his leg. "What bad luck!" the villagers exclaimed. "Your poor son! It's terrible. And how will you get your work done? You are too old to do it yourself."

"Good luck, bad luck. Who knows?" the old man said again, like a wise broken record. "My son has broken his leg. That is all I know."

Shortly thereafter, a war broke out in his country, and the government drafted all the able-bodied men from the village to go fight. The old man's son was spared since his leg was broken.

Bad luck, good luck, bad luck, good luck. This story can go on and on. Just as your own life.

If you are currently going through a stroke of bad luck, give it a minute. I will bet you a herd of wild horses that whatever circumstances you deem as bad or unwanted right now will directly pave the way for something wonderful. Something that would never have happened if you didn't go through the "bad" thing.

A blessing in disguise

When Herb and I ran the hostel in Mexico, a traveler named DeeDee was scheduled to start volunteering at the hostel on August 1. She had already arranged her personal travel plans around that date when an unforeseen issue required us to postpone her start date by two weeks. We felt terrible, but there was no other option.

When we messaged DeeDee with the news, she experienced, understandably, a mix of annoyance and anger. Travel plans would have to be changed again. Patience summoned. *Bad luck?*

LOST & FOUND

With the extra two weeks, she decided to stay longer in Guatemala before returning to Mexico to volunteer. During that extra time, she met someone special, a fellow world traveler. Sparks flew. They started dating. He came to visit the hostel while she volunteered, and then they traveled together around Mexico.

"It's the most meaningful relationship I've had in many years," she says. The start date setback turned out to be the biggest blessing in disguise. *Good luck?*

Judging or labeling any given situation creates misleading expectations at best and needless suffering at worst. Any given moment, event, or outcome is not inherently good or bad. It is always unfinished and inextricably connected to other moments. A work in progress. Zoom out far enough, wait a bit patiently, and you will see that there's a method to the madness.

Do you pause a movie in the middle of a tense fight scene where the hero appears to be losing and conclude, *Well, he's a goner!* No, you watch the movie until the end, enjoying the expected ups and downs, the unexpected twists and turns.

The movie of your life is constantly unfolding. A marathon screening in progress. Why pause or fixate on a hard moment, a seeming stroke of bad luck? Keep watching. The sad scenes will give way to something amazing. *I did not see that coming*, you'll say.

I am not suggesting you have to be happy when tragedy strikes. Loved ones passing away. Partners leaving. An illness arising. These painful lows are a natural part of living. And many of our most euphoric high points would quite literally not exist without the lows.

The gift of rejection

My (future) partner Herb got dumped at the beginning of the pandemic. I got dumped a few months later (by Mister Synchronicity in Chapter 2). Neither experience was particularly fun. But it did clear the way for some magic: we were both single at the same time. Both open to the possibility of exploring whether a new flirtation would evolve into something deeper.

Our exes gave us the beautiful gift of rejection. The pain of those rejections gave us the opportunity to further work on ourselves. I got to practice the art of loving and respecting myself more instead of less, so I would not have to play out that insecurity drama in my next relationship. Now after two incredible years together, a part of me wants to send Herb's ex-girlfriend a gift basket and thank-you card for setting him free.

Often what feels like not getting your way in the present is actually a priceless gift from your future. It's the universe or your higher self looking out for your best interest, redirecting you toward a path or a person you can't yet see.

But don't take my word for it. Take the Dalai Lama's:

> *Remember that sometimes not getting what you want is a wonderful stroke of luck.*

LOST & FOUND

The pandemic opened doors

One last example with universal relevance. The pandemic has altered the course of life for everyone on the planet. Many lives have been tragically ended by it, including my grandmother's.

The virus closed countless borders and many doors, especially for those in restrictive lockdowns. But it also opened new, unexpected doors. It motivated people to make big, positive changes in their lives. To end toxic relationships. Change jobs. Discover new passions and purposes.

Many jobs and training programs have now been moved entirely online, allowing people to enroll who would have had logistical or geographic barriers when everything was in person.

I'm not saying the pandemic is a good thing. Nor a bad thing. The labels are pointless. But the event itself has undeniably re-charted the course of many lives. *Good luck, bad luck. Who knows?*

Would you go up to a naked tree in winter and say, "The poor thing has lost all its leaves—how very sad!" Of course not. You know the leaves will return in a few months. The tree will inevitably blossom, good as new.

The same is true for humans. We are in a constant cycle of death and rebirth. Ups and downs. Pleasure and pain. At times the winter feels longer or harsher than we would like. But it always ends.

ALLA POLSKY

Sometimes when you're in a dark place you think you've been buried, but you've actually been planted. —Christine Caine

The next time life seemingly doesn't go your way, see what happens if you don't label it as a bad thing. What happens if you simply wait for the gift from your future to arrive.

16

A GIFT FROM A STRANGER IN MY PAST

A brief romance in Honduras taught me a lifetime of lessons on happiness

The following piece originally appeared in *Off Assignment*'s "Letter To A Stranger" section, in which you write a fake letter to someone real you met while traveling. Someone with whom a relatively brief encounter still continues to haunt you. I chose to write to a young man who gave me a priceless gift and reminded me what really matters.

To The Guy Who Gave Me Pirate Booty In Honduras
"Just don't write about *me!*" you said, minutes after we met.

A purely playful request, as what little I knew about you then would fail to captivate readers: Tall, Cute Guy Spotted At Coffee Shop In Roatán, Honduras.

The aforementioned male had towered over my MacBook and asked, with genuine interest, what was I working on? A book proposal, I said. I was a travel writer, or aspired to be.

I would get exactly zero writing done in your presence.

ALLA POLSKY

When I asked what brought you to the island of Roatán—aside from the views of a tropical paradise—you showed me photos I had never seen before. A small deep sea submarine, painted a cheerful Minion yellow, its portholes like cartoon eyes.

"It's a one-of-a-kind sub," you explained, "that aids in marine research and takes curious, non-claustrophobic civilians to record-setting depths." Yesterday you had plummeted (purposely) to 1,500 feet and waited for hours in cramped darkness with the sub's creator and pilot, hoping to spot a giant six-gill shark and other elusive creatures that only inhabit the deep. Your camera roll and still palpable excitement confirmed it was worth the wait.

I'll admit I barely noticed the scar on your shaved head. Too distracted by your stories, or perhaps by the crush I was developing. My friend T noticed it, though. Her resolve to work quietly in the corner had weakened at the mention of six-gill sharks and your Jules Vernean adventure.

"How'd you get the scar?" she asked. When you answered, my heart sank deeper than your submarine.

Four years ago, a baseball-sized tumor appeared in your brain. It was removed in a ten-hour surgery fit for *Grey's Anatomy*: the patient stays awake and talks so that doctors don't damage his speech function while extracting nearly ten percent of his brain!

After surgery you began a long course of chemo. A grad student at MIT at the time, and a self-described dork obsessed with data and technology, you wanted to learn everything you could about your tumor. So naturally you had it genetically sequenced, scanned, 3-D printed, and even molded into Christmas ornaments for family and friends. You gave a TED talk about the ordeal, using your own experience to advocate for open-sourcing patient data and a better system of sharing our medical records—our cellfies—across the global research community to accelerate learning and cures.

When it comes to attraction, I had always described my "type" as simply smart and funny. You were smart-and-funny on steroids.

But there was nothing funny about what you said next.

After years of clean scans, a routine check-up revealed a nasty glioblastoma, the most aggressive type of brain tumor. The cancer had returned. You needed another risky surgery, and even if it went well, glioblastomas are incurable. So you called up your closest friends and a week later you were here together in Roatán, ticking adventures off your bucket list. The deep-diving sub was one.

There are few times in my life when I can recall feeling more acutely that life is so royally un-fucking-fair. This remarkable guy sitting in front of me did not look or act sick, and even when his mouth wasn't smiling, his eyes were. My mind struggled to accept the facts. Yours, unfathomably, did not.

"So yeah, the surgery is next week," you said. "I don't know how much time I have left, but I'd rather spend it happy and enjoying every moment I can."

Is the bigger tragedy that people get cancer, I wondered, or that more people can't be happy while perfectly healthy? Why do we need the threat of death to remind us to cherish life?

ALLA POLSKY

You needed no reminders. Next on your Honduran bucket list? Hunting for pirate treasure. Today people associate the Bay Islands, Roatán being the largest, with world-class scuba diving and white sand beaches. But you taught me about their pirate-filled past. In the 1700s, Roatán was a safe haven for sea robbers in search of a hideout, both for themselves and their pillaged gold. It is rumored that treasure is still buried around these parts. So you and your friends hired a local guy with a boat to explore a nearby uninhabited island, armed with machetes and metal detectors.

Did my friend and I want to join the expedition? You were sweet enough to ask. I was unbelievably tempted but declined. I wanted you and your friends to have your bonding time. I did tell you some awful pirate jokes, though. What's a pirate's favorite sweater? ARRR-gyle!

We kept running into each other around town. Accidentally at first. Then intentionally. Our groups met up for dancing at Frank's, a beachfront bar with $1 tequila shots and the best reggaeton DJs in town.

You and I outlasted everyone on the dance floor.

The next day you went off on your treasure hunt while I scoured for the best dive school to start my PADI open water training. Only one week into a two-month stay on Roatán, I had already caught the diving bug.

You messaged me with news of pirate booty. After several amusing puns exchanged about assorted booty and who should bring their booty over where, I knew I'd be crazy to turn down the best kind of booty call a girl could get:

"Want to pick out some pirate glass for yourself?" you asked.

LOST & FOUND

You had not returned rich, but not empty-handed, either. The loot included a few 18th century coins, some rusty spikes presumed to be old ship parts, and many interesting fragments of glass, metal and rock. I chose a few small pieces that could double as meaningful mementos and easy travel companions.

On your last night in Roa, we sat outside gazing at stars. You must have felt fear and hope in nearly equal measure, though you tried to conceal the former. I kept searching for words of wisdom, something that didn't sound like a useless cliché. Words failed. I strummed "Peaceful Easy Feeling" by the Eagles on my ukulele instead.

"How old are you?" you kept asking when we first met. I kept deflecting until you played the cancer card. "Come on, it can't be *that* bad. And I know bad..." (This card had also proved handy in convincing your tired friends to take vodka shots.)

Okay, six years older isn't exactly cougar territory, but your nice round thirty made me feel old. What can I say? Girls get weird about their age after 30.

You would make it to 31. You died the day before my birthday. The sad news wouldn't reach me until a week later, but on that day I cried several times for no apparent reason. An overreaction to turning another year older, I figured. Another year of dead-end dating and dwindling fertility.

Was an island fling on your bucket list? I'll never know. And anyway, calling this thing a fling feels cheap. We had a real connection. But calling it anything more would be hyperbole.

A week after you left Honduras, you went into brain surgery and spent some nail-biting days in the ICU. Your friend was kind enough to send me updates while you recovered.

ALLA POLSKY

A few months later, you reached out to thank me for the good luck note I wrote just before your surgery. "You are such a lovely person and I hope you know that," you wrote back.

"Till the next time we end up in the same place."

Those would be your last words to me. I wish that we could have that next time. But mostly I just wish you had more time.

I replied too casually, trying to keep the mood light and breezy, not wanting to add any more heaviness to your life. "I'm so glad you're ok!" I wrote. "Takes one to know one, fellow lovely person. Keep searching for pirate booty."

That's right. My last words to you were pirate booty. Not my most poetic moment, but it's because I never fully believed that you could die. That we would need last words.

What I meant to say was, thank you. For sweeping into my life like a cool Caribbean breeze and reminding me what a privilege it is to keep aging. And what a treasure to meet people who seem to make time stop.

17

ACTUALLY USEFUL WAYS TO BE UNHAPPY

An unofficial guide to feeling our emotions

Emotions are like children. You don't want them driving the car, but you don't want to stuff them in the trunk, either.

I first heard this little nugget of wisdom during my yoga teacher training in Costa Rica. It also popped up in the movie *Thanks for Sharing* starring Mark Ruffalo. After an earnest 45-minute internet search, I failed to find the quote's original author. Let's misattribute it to Albert Einstein like most wise sayings.

As a society we are finally moving toward a point in our collective emotional development where it's acceptable—preferable even—to express emotions rather than shove them down and pretend like they don't exist. Yes, even for men.

But it's still a confusing, emotional time to be alive. Where's the sanity-preserving sweet spot between giving your feelings free rein (letting them drive the car) and pretending like they don't exist (stuffing them in the trunk)?

First let us acknowledge that not all feelings are created equal in our minds. We tend to judge, label and categorize them. Generally we like to feel good and prefer to avoid feeling bad. Even if someone has masochistic tendencies, deriving pleasure from pain, it's the same overarching pull toward feeling good. Freud called this the pain-pleasure principle. Our actions are motivated overwhelmingly by the desire to either move toward pleasure or away from pain.

We get attached to feelings we categorize as pleasurable. *I like feeling happy.* And we tend to avoid the feelings we label as painful or bad. *I don't like to feel sad, angry or scared.* Yet both sets of emotions have a very useful purpose to play in your personal growth. When you get upset or triggered by other people or events in your life, this is hugely valuable information. It's an opportunity to look inward and ask yourself *why*, rather than immediately pointing the blame at someone or something external.

I learned a solid lesson about misplaced blame when I first started teaching yoga. As a new instructor, I understandably felt insecure about my teaching abilities. Though I had done as much practice, study, and preparation as humanly possible, my imposter syndrome flared up during those first few classes. *You are a crappy yoga teacher, and everyone here knows it.* As if to confirm this fear on cue, while teaching my second class, a young woman in the front row suddenly stopped doing yoga. With twenty minutes of class remaining, she resolutely rolled up her mat and left.

LOST & FOUND

Oh my god, I thought to myself, *I am so bad at teaching that people are leaving in the middle of class.* I felt humiliated, rejected, and a little angry at this woman who couldn't even muster up the kindness to pretend my class was bearable like the other students. I somehow got through the final posture, Savasana, without losing my composure—or any more yogis. Since the rogue student's early departure, my energy had been split between teaching with presence and concealing my sadness. That sadness followed me around for the next few hours like a guided missile—until later that day when the woman who left early came up to me and said, "Thank you for a great class today! I loved it. I was sorry I had to leave early for a doctor's appointment."

Well, well. My bruised ego did not see that coming! Unable to hide my relief and amusement, I told her about the story I had made up in my head after she left class. We both had a good laugh, and I got a priceless lesson about my thoughts and emotions. Sometimes *neither* of them are rooted in reality. Yet they both convincingly drag me down to their fictional pity party.

Since I was already feeling insecure, my mind processed one student's early departure as evidence of my inferior teaching skills. This made-up story in my head instantly made me feel like crap. I was lucky to be blatantly proven wrong, but how many other times did I ruin my mood based on a mistaken assumption or complete mental delusion that would never be corrected?

I was fully ready to believe that I was the world's worst yoga teacher, and ready to let those negative feelings drive my teaching career into a ditch. It was a much-needed wakeup call not only about the consuming power my thoughts and feelings have over me, but how unreliable those thoughts and feelings can be in the first place. Now when I catch myself weaving a negative tale in my mind about myself or someone else, I notice the negative emotion that accompanies it and ask if either are serving me in any way. The answer is No more often than a yogi says *Om*.

Locking them in the trunk

Many of us are inadvertently taught in childhood to suppress our emotions. "Suck it up. Big boys don't cry," an exhausted father might have said in an attempt to stop his son's tantrum in public.

For girls there is not the same stigma toward crying, but most of us have heard the phrase "Don't be so emotional" by the time we reach the first signs of womanhood. If we are quick to raise our voice or shed tears, it must either be that hormonal time of the month or we are being "too sensitive" in general.

The subtext is that there's a limit to how much negative emotion either gender is allowed to feel or display. (And there's a subtle hierarchy toward certain emotions by gender: as women we are generally allowed to cry and be sad but not be *angry*—that is completely unladylike. For men it's the opposite: if you *must* feel something, get angry, punch a wall. At least that's manly. Just don't be a sissy and *cry*.)

Is it any wonder we end up shoving negative emotions down and concealing them if at all possible? We internalize this as the optimal way to deal with feelings. Shoving them down gets us love and acceptance. Showing them makes us look weak or unstable, and burdens our loved ones. We shove them so far down and for so long that we start to forget those emotions are even there.

I lived in New York City for six years. Though I often felt lonely, overworked, and anxious, I remember crying maybe once. I had this desired image of myself as someone who had her shit together. Not a "hot mess" kind of girl.

Nearly every day, I would either go for a run, take a yoga class, or have drinks with friends to unwind from stress. Some days all three. If you are thinking that yoga and running are much healthier ways to relieve stress than a night at the bar, it's not so black and white.

I used all three activities to lock my kids in the trunk, emotionally speaking. To push down feelings of stress, anxiety, and loneliness. I wanted to feel less, not more. At one point I was running 5 to 10 miles a day, literally running away from my problems. Trying to escape them or cover them up temporarily with endorphins. But they were always waiting for me back at home.

Sure, technically a run or a yoga class is better for you than say, heroin, as a way to relieve stress. But the healthiest of all would be to directly address the underlying source of that stress, rather than temporarily numb it with things like exercise, alcohol, movies, casual sex, and so on.

If a teapot is whistling on the stove, you can raise the lid to momentarily relieve the pressure. But unless you address the underlying issue—the fire heating it up—the pressure will continue to build and the teapot will inevitably scream again.

Avoidance tactics are essentially a short-term fix. Eventually those emotions *will* erupt again, like the teapot, and usually at the most inopportune moments. Your life car will hit a tiny speed bump or a gaping pothole, and that trunk will pop right open. Perhaps at the office during an important meeting, like mine did once. Ah, crying at work. Such a millennial cliché.

If you shove emotional pain down long enough, it eventually cries out in the form of physical pain in the body. In case you needed another reason to let it out of the trunk.

Letting them drive

Real life examples of handing your emotions the car keys are often easier to spot than of locking them away in the trunk. It's the toddlers and Karens of the world having a meltdown in a grocery store. The angry guy punching a wall, or punching his partner.

Expressing emotions is preferable to ignoring them. But letting those emotions control you to the point where you needlessly hurt others or yourself? That's a car wreck waiting to happen.

I recently watched a movie called *The Mustang* about a prison rehabilitation program where inmates train wild horses. In one powerful scene, a group therapy session takes place. A psychologist asks each inmate, "How long from the thought of the crime to the actual crime?" The answers are haunting. "Ten seconds." "Five seconds." "A split-second." They then share how long they've been in prison. 17 years. 18 years.

LOST & FOUND

"First-degree murder since I was 14," says a man who looks to be in his seventies. How long from the thought of his crime to the act of it? "Uh, well, just spontaneous," he replies, grasping the tragic irony. A few seconds of anger and rage would define and imprison the rest of these men's lives. This may seem like a very extreme example of what can happen when we let our emotions drive the car, but it's a nightmarish reality for too many criminals and their victims.

How many of us have said something hurtful to someone we loved during a heated argument and instantly regretted it? Or done something we wished we could undo? That anger seems to come out of nowhere. Yet most often it has been festering in our subconscious or held in our bodies for a long time. At its core anger is actually sadness that had no place to go for a maddeningly long time.

Emotional regulation is so crucial to our daily existence, and yet so rarely taught when we are growing up—perhaps because many of our teachers and caregivers are still struggling to master it themselves.

Putting them lovingly in the backseat

So if it's not ideal to let emotions drive, nor to lock them in the trunk, where is the healthy middle ground? Strap them in to the backseat, like you would a child passenger you love and want to protect from harm. Give your feelings a secure space to express themselves, with a safe distance from the steering wheel. Give them your awareness and attention without judging them, without labeling them as bad or good, nor focusing on one particular emotion so intently that you fail to notice everything else going on inside you and around you.

In the case of major grief, heartbreak, or trauma, this is easier said than done. You do not have to *like* the emotions you are feeling, but can you at least love the person who is feeling them? Can you hold space for yourself without judgment?

Ironically, the moment you are fully okay with whatever you are feeling in the moment—not trying to expedite a future reality when you feel better—is the moment you start to feel better exactly where you are.

The car is built to move

All emotions, the ones you would normally label as pleasurable, painful or neutral—all the way from rapturous joy to deep depression—are designed to *move*.

E-motion.

We are not supposed to hold on to them indefinitely. That's how traumas form. Traumas are emotions that got stuck in your body or in your subconscious mind, sometimes without your conscious awareness. Painful memories or unpleasant feelings were trapped and held on to rather than being allowed to be felt, moved, and healed.

Not everyone has what therapists call "big T Traumas"—deeply traumatic events like being abused, wounded in a horrible accident, or losing a loved one at a young age. But all of us have "little t traumas" that have stacked up over the years, those little hurts and rejections from family, friends, romantic partners, and society in general.

LOST & FOUND

My partner Herb has seen transformational healing in his clients by combining somatic (body) and hypnotic (mind) therapy techniques. When Herb offered me a session, I didn't have any specific traumas to work on, at least not consciously. But I have been struggling with psoriasis on my scalp, an autoimmune skin condition, since around the age of 12. I wondered if his therapeutic approach could help me find a psychological link or emotional trigger for this physical ailment. The technique seems especially effective for traumas that have been repressed or do not have a conscious memory attached.

My session begins with Herb asking me to bring up the emotion associated with my psoriasis flare-ups. They cause my scalp to itch or burn almost constantly and create embarrassing white flakes. I bring up that pain, irritation, and shame while keeping my eyes fixed on various points. About ten minutes later, I am sobbing. I don't know exactly why the tears started, but soon vivid memories come flooding back. Memories I had completely forgotten about, little t traumas from my childhood. Like being bullied in sixth grade gym class, a mean blond girl and her mean boyfriend hurling a volleyball at my head on purpose. The physical pain from that ball is nothing compared to the emotional pain I immediately push down. *Do NOT let them see you cry*, I remember commanding myself as a mix of sadness and anger courses through my body. My middle school self is unable to comprehend how someone could hate me so much for absolutely no reason.

After some more crying in Herb's office, a bit of shaking, and a fit of laughter that makes me sound like a lunatic, another memory appears in my mind. Sixth grade cafeteria. I find a surprise handwritten note inside my packed lunch: *We don't want you to sit at our table anymore.* I suspect it's from one girl in particular, someone I once considered a close friend. But the note says "We". Do *all* of my supposed friends secretly hate me? Again, the rejection by my peers is more than I can handle emotionally at the time. I push the pain down, act like I don't care, and completely forget about the experience for nearly three decades. Now it is ready to come out. The car is built to move, after all. My emotional trunk has finally popped open. It feels both painful and liberating to let that baggage out at last.

I cry for nearly an hour in my partner's plush therapy chair. These hurtful suppressed memories are interspersed with moments of levity. Sudden fits of laughter. My young self didn't know how to process the feelings of rejection and cruelty from her peers. So she pushed them down so deep that I had completely forgotten these events occurred. Until I finally had the tools and emotional strength to process them and let them go.

All things considered, I had a pretty great childhood. My parents and sister were loving and supportive. I did well in school. Eventually I found true friends who didn't try to give me concussions in gym class or follow the *Mean Girls* script during lunch. Yet I was not immune to those little traumas buried so deep in my subconscious that I had lost all memory of them. I now understand why psoriasis began to flare up in middle school, with its social stress and peer rejection. I am hopeful that more shadow work can fully clear my scalp, and clear my subconscious of any other latent traumas.

The desire to avoid or move away from pain is natural, so we tend to shove those big and little traumas down. As children we try to forget them or we act out. As adults we drown them out with alcohol, with exercise, with work. With binge eating, binge watching, binge traveling. Sometimes all of the above, which was my personal grown-up trauma avoidance strategy for nearly two decades. It failed miserably. Because what you resist truly does persist. If you lock your unwanted feelings in the trunk of your life car, whether consciously or unconsciously, they will continue to weigh you down.

Pain is powerful fuel for growth

The most inspirational stories often come from someone overcoming unbelievable odds or rising above a horrific experience. These heroes become inspirational role models. Some even decide to dedicate their lives to helping others overcome the same types of obstacles. For example, there are war veterans who conquer their own PTSD and start organizations to help their fellow soldiers heal through creative avenues like art therapy, improv acting, or surfing. There are parents who have suffered the unfathomable grief of losing a child and later go on to lead support groups that help other parents cope. Recovering alcohol and drug addicts often go on to mentor and guide others who are trapped in the throes of addiction.

You would never wish for your traumas and life struggles, but since you got stuck with them, they can actually be a huge source of personal growth for yourself and a source of inspiration and healing for others. In other (cheesier) words, when life hands you traumatic lemons, see if you can turn them into traumanade. Two spoonfuls of sugar, a dash of depression, and a sprinkling of happy tears. (Random fun fact to share at your next dinner party: the chemical composition of tears shed from joy is actually different than tears shed out of sadness.)

Clinical scientists are even starting to find that depression can be a natural, beneficial process on the way to spiritual and personal growth. In a powerful TEDx Talk, Dr. Lisa Miller recounts her personal experience with depression as she and her husband struggled to conceive a child.[9] In going through the painful ordeal, she watched as her depression directly paved the way to her spiritual awakening—and to becoming the kind of mother she was always meant to be. Her clinical research echoes her personal experience: brain scans of depressed people with spiritual beliefs show immense strengthening of the regions previously thought to deteriorate with depression.

In his bestselling books, Eckhart Tolle attests that suffering is often a prerequisite to spiritual awakening. He himself was deeply depressed and even contemplating taking his own life when he had a consciousness shift that instantly sparked his awakening. If depression had not dragged him down to the depths of saying, "I just can't live with myself anymore," *The Power of Now* may never have been written and gone on to help millions.

LOST & FOUND

Chapter 20 will explore this topic further and answer the burning question of exactly how much suffering (if any) is required for a spiritual awakening.

If you fight it, you feed it

On a global scale there is no shortage of things to feel unhappy and distressed about today. Wars, famine, genocide, deadly diseases, environmental disasters, political corruption, poverty, racism. Just to name a few.

Some days it all makes me want to crawl into an air-conditioned cave and hide. Other days I feel hopeful and energized. I try to abide by Wayne Dyer's mantra: "Everything you are against weakens you. Everything you are for empowers you." In other words, concentrating my energy and actions toward fighting *against* something, which usually involves hateful or negative emotions, leaves me drained and only feeds the collective hatred. In contract, channeling my energy toward positive issues and inspiring change leaves me feeling empowered and fuels love on a collective level. This isn't just hippie-dippy talk for a fantasy world. It's a practical law of the universe with tangible benefits for your personal happiness and society's collective sanity.

Here is a practical example to demonstrate the subtle difference between being in the predominant energy of FOR something versus AGAINST something. I used to be a political junkie. I spent hours watching political talk shows, reading political news, following national and local elections, even donating money to candidates' campaigns. But often my motivation came from a place of fear of the other side winning.

ALLA POLSKY

I wasn't so much rooting for my candidate as voting against the other party. During the 2016 election for U.S. President, when Donald Trump won, I felt distraught and hopeless for months. Many of my close friends and family did, too. Did our collective depression do any good for the country or for our own personal well-being? Nope. It fueled more hatred, more division, more unhappiness.

I'm not saying I needed to be happy with my country's choice for president. Only that being against him and against the reality of his new job title served no purpose. Eventually I burned out on the negative news coverage and tuned out his toxic Tweets. Instead I turned my attention to the positive side effects of his presidency. He had inspired a new generation to get involved, run for political office, and shift the demographic makeup of Congress to be more racially diverse, more gender balanced, and younger. When I needed a political news fix, I watched documentaries about inspiring new leaders instead of ones about Trump's corruption.

Martin Luther King Jr. famously said, "Darkness cannot drive out darkness. Only light can do that. Hate cannot drive out hate, only love can do that." He succeeded in growing a massive civil rights movement because he led with the energy of love and empowerment, not the energy of hate and cynicism. It was the same with Gandhi fighting for India's independence. He didn't fight with violence and anger, but rather advocated for peace through his words and actions. It spread the frequency of love and hope, not hate and negativity. Nelson Mandela took a similar stance in the movement to end apartheid in South Africa.

LOST & FOUND

Mother Teresa said, "I will never attend an anti-war rally. If you have a peace rally, invite me." It may seem like simple semantics, being anti-war versus pro-peace, but the energy of them is completely different. If you signal to the universe that you derive satisfaction from fighting *against* something, it will give you more of that thing in the world, so that you can keep fighting. Declaring a war on drugs has only created more drugs in the world, more people in prison, more people hooked on drugs.

The bestselling book *The Secret: The Law of Attraction* explains that the universe doesn't understand "No." If you focus on the negative, on the things you *don't* want, the things you are against, for example dwelling on your fear of getting a parking ticket—*I hope I don't get a parking ticket*—the universe will hear that you are calling in a parking ticket. *What's that? She keeps fixating on a parking ticket. Give this woman what she wants!*

Another example is the feminist movement. Being anti-men and railing against the patriarchy is a different energy than being pro-women, pro-equality, and celebrating the strides women are making. The former leaves you feeling angry and drained while also alienating men from wanting to join the cause. The latter is inclusive and leaves you feeling empowered and optimistic.

For years I followed the writing of a talented female blogger. She mainly wrote about the woes of modern dating, the disappointing men she encountered on dating apps, and the struggles of being a single woman in your thirties. At a conscious level, her aim was to celebrate single women in a society that seems to pity and stigmatize them. But unconsciously, she was signaling to the universe that she derives some satisfaction, passion, and endless writing material from remaining single. She went on to publish a whole book about it.

I was single for a decade, so I can certainly relate and commiserate with her perspective. But I also wonder if it is fueling her singlehood by identifying so strongly with her single status and writing about it with a predominantly negative, angry energy of what she is against. During my unattached decade, the handful of articles I published about being single were mainly in the energy of optimism, personal growth, and excitement to call in my partner. When my writing tone veered toward pessimism and anger, I treated it like a venting journaling exercise and chose not to publish it.

The best thing we can do for our own happiness and for the collective good is to make this subtle shift in how we frame our beliefs and behaviors. Tip the scales toward championing what we love in the world, rather than fixating on what or who we hate about it.

A final example that may seem harmless but actually caused me considerable unhappiness: competitive sports. Throughout my twenties and early thirties, I was a serious sports fan. College football and basketball in particular (Go Stanford!), but also NFL and NBA (Go Dallas Cowboys! Go Mavs!). I spent hundreds of hours watching games, anxiously yelling at the TV screen when my team was losing, then actively hating the rival team that beat us for days. I even spent thousands of dollars traveling to watch important games in person with friends who were fellow fanatics. The distress of losing a Rose Bowl tournament was compounded after taking a cross-country flight and time off from work to root for my team.

Competitive sports were a huge part of my life back then, and I wasn't consciously aware that it caused me more suffering than joy. I regularly participated in fantasy football leagues and March Madness brackets, taking extra delight in not only being part of a mostly male-dominated world, but beating them at their game. Sure, the winning part felt nice. But those highs were inevitably offset by the lows of losing, and the overall stress of watching live games, with so much emotionally invested in the outcome.

It wasn't a conscious decision, but as I discovered less competitive passions like yoga, travel, scuba diving, and photography, I gradually lost all interest in watching sports. There didn't need to be a winner and a loser anymore. In fact, I started feeling more like a winner every day, not missing those days of stressing over the outcomes of political elections and sporting events, or being angry about world events I couldn't change. Go Happiness!

18

ACTUALLY USEFUL HAPPINESS RESEARCH FINDINGS

I scoured all the books, research papers & TED Talks my brain could handle

Ever notice how most studies about happiness tell you things you already knew—or could have safely assumed without paying someone thousands of dollars in research grants to corroborate?

Scientists have found that partners who talk to each other are happier than those who are dating mimes! (silent gasp)

This just in: Eating healthier, exercising, and getting more sleep also makes you more happy!

Yeah, thanks, overpaid people in lab coats. I would file most findings on happiness under the No shit, Sherlock section of my brain.

My personal favorite stupidly obvious finding from a real research study: People who ate lunch at their desk felt less happy about their job than workers who ate lunch—wait for it—*at the beach!*

LOST & FOUND

I know, right? Who could have guessed? Unless your occupation is lifeguard or dolphin, it's surprisingly hard to sneak in a beach break in the middle of the work day. For six years I worked two blocks away from a beautiful waterfront in sight of the Statue of Liberty. I can count on one finger the number of lunches I ate outside.

You might be wondering why I bother to read reports on the science of happiness when they appear to make me 50% less happy and 200% more agitated. Well, I come from a family with a multi-generational history of anxiety, depression, and a general predisposition toward overreacting (The Holocaust didn't help). So perusing the latest happiness hacks is my version of a beach break.

Before we get to the findings that have actually surprised me in a good way, let's first address an odd fact about the more obvious findings: If we instinctively know these things to be true—that spending more time with our loved ones, or taking a walk in nature, or getting more sleep and eating fewer cheeseburgers, will make us more happy—why aren't we doing them more often?

In truth, I have no idea. At least my rational brain does not. The disconnect is at the subconscious level. Most of us are not intentionally sabotaging our health, our relationships, our stress levels. It's happening below the conscious cognitive level, in the subconscious mind which is estimated to control a whopping 95% of our actions, desires, fears, and beliefs—without us consciously realizing it.

Most happiness research mistakenly tries to plead its case to our conscious rational mind, that feeble 5%, feeding it reasonable sounding suggestions like "go eat lunch outside" and "exercise at least 20 minutes a day." It misses the underlying reasons we avoid doing these things in the first place. At a deeper, more compelling level beneath the rational mind, we actually believe that NOT doing these things will make us more happy than doing them.

In the case of my sad, solitary desk lunches, I was either too pressed for time to leave (taking a fancy outdoor lunch might add the stress of feeling less prepared for a meeting), or I didn't feel like eating alone in public (most of my colleagues ate at their desk as well). Plus, lunching at your desk makes you appear like a dedicated, hardworking employee who puts her job ahead of personal needs. Double-win! At least that's the belief system I had unconsciously bought into.

When I look back on all those years I spent cooped up inside an office building, I suspect there is still some lingering trauma around it. It may seem like a relatively harmless circumstance, working in an office, but it sparked several anxiety attacks over the years. After I quit my job and my city life, I swore I would never again work full-time in an office building.

I became a freelancer, taking on predominantly short-term, remote projects with former employers and clients. I was lucky enough to have this privilege after building a reputation for great work spanning more than a decade. I have worked from Greek islands, Moroccan beaches, and Guatemalan lakes. I am simply one of over 35 million digital nomads who didn't need to read the research findings to know that this lifestyle would make me happier (and be vastly more affordable than the cost of living in the U.S.)

LOST & FOUND

Without further ado, here are some of the more surprising studies on happiness, backed by serious science, including ones that shed additional light on why I was so miserable at the office.

Happy dirt: Most people know from experience that nature can lift our spirits. The vitamin D from sunshine, the calming effects of oceans and forests. Now researchers in England have discovered that breathing in the smell of dirt acts as a natural antidepressant, thanks to a harmless bacteria commonly found in soil.[10] *Mycobacterium vaccae* affects your brain like antidepressant drugs, stimulating the release of serotonin. Cancer patients treated with this bacteria reported increases in their quality of life. Just imagine what playing outside in the dirt could do for healthy people.

Learning high: Learning new information activates the brain's dopamine-producing reward system in the same way as money or food.[11] Whether or not the information is actually useful, our brains are Curious Marvins, treating new info like a valuable reward. So learning random facts (like this one) can make you feel as happy as finding cash or eating something tasty. The brain can't tell the difference.

Sad songs: It seems counter-intuitive, but listening to sad music has been shown to make people *less* sad, by regulating their emotions and increasing feelings of consolation.[12] As a moody teenager listening to sappy country songs about heartbreak, I thought I was intentionally wallowing in my loneliness and self-pity. But it turns out the sad songs were helping me process my own pain, rather than pushing it down and pretending it didn't exist. As with most things, there is value in moderation—you might lose a few friends after an hour of blasting Johnny Cash's "Hurt" on infinite loop.

Happy life, happy wife: Despite the conventional wisdom of "happy wife, happy life", the reverse is far more accurate. A massive research study on 11,000 couples found that by far the biggest predictor of happiness in a romantic relationship is whether you are happy *outside* of your relationship.[13] It's not your partner's responsibility to make you happy—it's yours. This single notion trumps every factor we typically associate with happiness in a relationship (having an attractive, financially stable, intelligent mate who shares your interests and values, etc). When two psychologically healthy, reasonably happy humans get together, there is a very high likelihood that they will stay together, happily.

Happy goodbyes: In a multi-year study of working men in Germany, researchers found that husbands who kissed their wives before leaving for work lived an average of five years longer (and earned more money) than those who did not.[14] Okay, maybe this finding isn't all that surprising. If you genuinely love your partner and domestic life is good, you are probably more affectionate and in a better mood when you leave the house. Living with someone you actually like lowers stress, thereby increasing health and happiness. If you want to live longer, why force yourself to eat kale when you could simply spend more time smooching?

To recap, activities like rolling in the dirt, learning random facts, getting frisky in doorways, and listening to Beethoven's maudlin Moonlight Sonata can genuinely make us happier. One surprising behavior that tends to bring us *less* happiness? The pursuit of happiness itself:

Happiness hangover: There is a growing body of research suggesting that the actual pursuit of happiness can make us less happy overall. Western societies are especially obsessed with happiness and how to cram more of it into every aspect of life, from work to relationships to alone time. Ironically, this constant pressure and fixation of happiness has been linked to feeling more lonely, more anxious about the passage of time, and more disconnected from enjoying simple, everyday pleasures.[15] It's a bit like going to a comedy show where the comic asks the audience in between each joke, "Was that funny? Are you entertained? I sure hope I'm funny!" Instant laugh-killer. If you're constantly asking yourself "Am I happy?" you will come up with plenty of reasons not to be.

The other culprit is attaching our happiness to external factors, things we wish we had or perceive we lack. If only I could get that relationship, that pay raise, that next trip, that better beach body, THEN I would be happy. But as Harvard psychology professor Dan Gilbert's research shows, getting these things gives us a momentary surge in happiness and then inevitably wears off.[16] As a species, we humans are terrible at predicting what will make us happy in the future.

Is the key takeaway here that we should banish the H-word from our vocabulary and just live our lives? Not entirely. There is also a growing body of research showing something uplifting: when we shift the happiness focus from ourselves to others, meaning we try to make *others* happy instead of ourselves, we get the biggest happiness boost. It's like a cosmic commission from the universe:

Give happily: Countless studies have shown that spending money on others or simply doing nice things for others makes us happier than spending that same amount of time or money on ourselves. This isn't that surprising. What IS surprising is how much happier it makes you (considerably), and how little you need to give of your time or money to get that jolt of happiness (very little). Research has shown that anonymously feeding the parking meter of a stranger gives you more happiness than feeding your own.[17] We're talking a few coins here.

Years ago I felt particularly sad on one Monday morning during my train commute to the office. It wasn't a typical Case of the Mondays. It was my birthday. I felt sadness for the extra year in my age, loneliness for still being single, and lameness for spending the day at work. Suddenly I noticed a distressed woman fumbling with her Metro card. She couldn't get it to swipe properly to open the turnstile onto the subway platform, and the train was now arriving. Without hesitation, I swiped my own card for her and guided her through the entrance.

LOST & FOUND

That swipe cost me two dollars and taught me a priceless lesson about my own happiness. We rode the train together for about ten minutes. It was her first time in New York, hence the confusion entering the subway. I gave her some sightseeing recommendations. She tried to give me cash for the train fare. I refused. "Pay it forward if you like," I suggested, "There are plenty of people who could use a random act of kindness in this town." By the time the train pulled up at my stop, I no longer felt sad or sorry for myself. That momentary shift in my attention, away from my own problems, was completely unplanned. But it completely worked.

I walked into my office with a genuine smile. My coworkers figured it was the birthday glow, not knowing about the stranger who had helped me out of a birthday slump by allowing me to help her.

> *The surest way to be happy is to seek happiness for others.* —Martin Luther King, Jr.

It seems that Dr. King could have saved happiness researchers a lot of time and money. Psychologists are not entirely sure why this altruism thing works so well and so consistently. But some theorize that it's about our basic psychological need to feel close to others.

That could help explain why I felt happy on a stuffy, windowless six-hour bus ride through Guatemala and felt sad on a gorgeous white-sand beach in the Philippines. On the bus I chatted with a motorcycle-riding grandmother from Canada the entire time. We were like old friends by the end. On the beautiful beach I was alone, when I didn't want to be.

As long as we fixate on our own pursuit of happiness, or perceived lack thereof, it will continue to elude us. And if we attribute our own inner happiness to things outside of ourselves, like other people or gorgeous places or higher salaries, what happens when those external things change or disappear? In one more promising case of research, there is a happiness hack that seems almost too simple to be true:

Happier default setting: We all have a personal "happiness set point", a sort of default factory setting in our brain for how happy we normally are. Over time, we will return to this same set point even after a happiness surge from winning the lottery or a happiness plummet from being paralyzed in a horrible accident.[18] Some people have default set points that are much higher than others—genetics accounts for 50% of your happiness set point level. But the other 50% can be changed. Remarkably, meditation has been shown to literally rewire your brain to be more happy than your genetics naturally allow for.[19] And the effects can be enjoyed in a matter of days, not years or decades. For people with cranky genes like some members of my family (okay, me), this could be a game-changer.

I avoided meditation for years, not seeing the point nor seeing results until I started dating Herb (see Chapter 21). Once I committed to a daily seated practice, I quickly understood what all the fuss was about.

LOST & FOUND

If you meditate for long enough, you may notice your mood shifting from happy and calm to agitated and angry to bored and antsy, all during one seated practice. Nothing in the external environment will have changed. You are still sitting on a pillow with your eyes closed. But suddenly you feel the waves of changing emotions. Where did they come from? You realize they are arising from within and receding within. Your mind is controlling most of your emotions. The outside world you blame for your sadness, or award credit for your happiness, is an illusion.

There is groundbreaking research demonstrating the unbelievable benefits of training our minds to stay in the present (not straying to the past or the future, but observing reality as it actually unfolds, which is the central aim of meditation):

Happier in the moment: Dr. Matthew Killingsworth, creator of the massive global research project Track Your Happiness, tracked the daily lives of 15,000 people all around the world using a mobile app.[20] The goal was to capture real-time, moment-to-moment happiness levels and how different activities or experiences impacted our moods. The most surprising finding centered on mind-wandering. Participants were frequently asked, "Are you thinking about something other than what you're currently doing?" For the moments they answered "yes," signifying that their mind had wandered away from the present moment, their self-reported happiness level *dropped*.

On the whole, we feel less happy when our mind strays away from whatever we happen to be doing right now—even if we happen to be doing something unpleasant, like commuting to work. Even when our mind wanders to a more pleasant topic, we report being less happy than if we had stayed present with our boring drive to the office. The researchers found this mind-blowing, as do I. They also found that on average, people's minds stray about 47% of the time. That means we spend half of our day making ourselves less happy simply by *thinking*. It's a perfect segue into the next chapter and the last section of this book.

PART V: FINDING ENLIGHTENMENT

I have read millions of words from dozens of spiritual texts. They have confused me, frustrated me, uplifted me, and changed me at my core. The following is my humble attempt to clarify the confusing and minimize the frustration. To accelerate your own spiritual scavenger hunt toward Awakening, Enlightenment, Illumination, Liberation, Oneness, Higher Consciousness, or whatever you prefer to call it.

19

THE MOST BORING SPIRITUAL AWAKENING EVER

That time I "pierced the veil" from my office

The first time I felt a distinct shift in my consciousness, I wasn't in a yoga class or at a meditation retreat. I wasn't tripping on a psychedelic, nor even watching a majestic sunrise from a mountain top.

I was at the office. Sitting at my desk in front of my computer, like I had done on every weekday and too many weekends for the past two years.

On that particular afternoon, I felt overworked and resentful at all the leisure hours this job had stolen from me. So in a small moment of defiance, I began browsing Reddit at work. A link to a strange online book called *The Present* caught my eye, and I started reading it at my desk instead of reviewing research reports for a client.

The book used simple language to talk about complex things. I was still several years away from discovering Eckhart Tolle's *The Power of Now* and Ram Dass' *Be Here Now*. The following words introduced me to the powerful gift that is the present moment:

> *The more you live in the present, the more fulfilling life gets. Time will slow down; you will see the magic and wonder of life you saw as a child, and you will experience it without the ignorance and all the negative emotions of childhood.* — GlobalTruthProject.com

I binge-read the entire online text in about an hour. When I finished reading and looked beyond my computer screen, the office looked different. Brighter and shinier somehow. Perhaps I felt that way inside and projected it outward. Suddenly I saw everything with fresh eyes. The industrial windows in my office. The exposed pipes on the ceiling. The coworkers I shared the space with. All of it suddenly seemed *beautiful*.

I glanced out of my office into the hallway. People appeared to be gliding through the halls like ballet dancers. There was a rhythm to their movement that seemed almost choreographed. Not in a predictable way, simply graceful and effortless.

If this had happened to someone else and they described it to me in the same way, my inner skeptic would have thought, *Oh come on. Too cheesy to be true—unless someone slipped a micro-dose of LSD into your coffee this morning.* But it happened to me, without any drugs, and I felt like my eyes were truly open for the first time. I didn't yet have the spiritual vocabulary to understand what was happening. I only knew that it felt awesome. Absolutely nothing in my external environment had changed. It was the same drab office, the same tired colleagues. But inside something had shifted. This sometimes cynical New Yorker was in a sudden state of bliss.

I sensed that reading those words about being present had sparked the shift in consciousness. Perhaps not merely the words themselves but the energy behind them. I also sensed that if I had read them last year or even yesterday, they would not have had the same effect.

I glided next door to my friend Kerin's office. She was technically my manager at the time, less technically my closest friend in New York, and undoubtedly my "work wife" (a purely platonic label, in case Herb is reading this).

Kerin sat at her desk on a phone call. I already adored her as a friend and admired her as a colleague, but now I saw in her a deeper light. She radiated pure love. I was grateful that my glowing friend was occupied, because there was no way I could explain what was happening to me. She would think I was nuts. A part of me wondered the same.

I smiled at her and shook my head to say, *It's not important, I'll come back after your call.* It was important in a way I couldn't fully describe. Like a butterfly flapping its wings is important. I fluttered around the office with a goofy grin on my face. I smiled at everyone. I felt genuinely happy to be there, a contentment you couldn't fake. In that moment I didn't want to be anywhere else or doing anything else. It was pure presence.

LOST & FOUND

My mini awakening lasted maybe five minutes. The blissful state began to dissipate when I returned to my desk to a slew of new emails. But the veil had been pierced. I had glimpsed what was possible. A different slice of reality, one more constant and pure, untainted by my changing moods, thoughts and expectations. I wouldn't know it for another few weeks, but a seed had been planted on that day. And it wouldn't stay buried for long.

A few weeks later, I quit that job, sublet my apartment, and booked a one-way flight to Thailand. It was the unofficial start of my spiritual journey. On the surface it was a backpacking trip through Southeast Asia. But inside that overstuffed backpack was a hunch that I was not meant to spend ten hours a day inside an office for the rest of my life. On that big adventure abroad, I discovered a love for yoga and for traveling solo, both of which would change the course of my life in the years to come.

The trip had started with a mini awakening in the office, and it concluded with another subtle shift in my consciousness. Nearing the end of that three-month journey, I stood on a beach in Bali. The sun was setting, as it did every night. Some days it lit up the sky with a parade of pastels. Other days it set behind clouds without much fanfare. But regardless of the weather conditions, the local islanders would stop what they were doing, sit along the shore, and watch the sun sink into the ocean. Kids ate homemade popsicles. Stray dogs curled up in the sand.

In my New Yorker days, any description of watching a sunset would have sounded like a total cliché. *So cheesy*, I would think again. I had worked straight through hundreds of sunsets, often not leaving the office until dark. But standing on this Balinese beach, I felt that same shift again, the one that had lured me here in the first place. In that moment there was nowhere else I wanted to be. Nothing was needed to make me happier. Yes, I had upgraded the scenery from drab office to tropical paradise. But I had also upgraded my inner hardware to be able to fully appreciate such a moment. To be practically moved to tears by the simple joy and perfection of a sunset.

I wasn't the only one delighting in this simple joy. The predominantly local crowd around me had so little by Western standards, and yet they seemed genuinely happier than many people I knew back home. Those go-getters were too busy to watch a sunset. Too distracted to really *see* it, even if they could find the time to look. I had been one of them for years.

What had I truly seen that day in the office for the first time? The world as it actually is. Hidden in plain sight, obscured by the constant chatter of my mind. Even the most mundane things become enchanting when you remove the judgmental filter of your thinking brain, the part of you that labels things as boring or ugly or repetitive. I suppose enchanting is a judgment, too, albeit a pleasing one. I am labeling what I experienced with words now, but at the time I simply experienced.

We tend to romanticize spiritual awakenings. Expecting or awaiting some grand epiphany where the clouds part and a choir of angels congratulates you on reaching Enlightenment. My consciousness shift was so uneventful that I had no plans to ever tell anyone about it, let alone write about it. For eight years it remained my little secret. Then one day Herb and I, being spiritual nerds, were discussing shifts in consciousness at the dinner table. I said, "I think I had one of those at the office." He found my tale extraordinary, precisely because it was so ordinary on the surface. He told me of a similar experience he had while living in Ukraine during a brief meditation in his apartment. It made me realize that boring spiritual awakenings might be more common than dramatic ones. The person next to you has no idea that you are high on higher consciousness, piercing the veil of what we normally consider to be "reality." On the outside, everything is the same. On the inside, nothing is the same.

I wasn't looking to awaken on that particular day. I was just trying to get through another workday. But that five-minute shift in my consciousness set off a chain reaction of events that turned my life upside down. Or rightside up, to be more exact. I had been on the wrong path, not following my inner compass toward joy, until that tiny shift created seismic changes in my world to re-orient my purpose. It nudged me out into the world, toward my deeper purpose, toward my partner and new friends, toward this book, and toward a truer version of myself.

If you find yourself waiting for a grand vision or outwardly mystical experience to signal your awakening, you might miss it or doubt its significance when it comes. Not to worry, though. Once the seed has been planted in your consciousness, you will continue to get those little knowings, glimpses and shifts in awareness. Ignore the whispers long enough, and eventually they will start to shout. MAYBE THAT TIME IS NOW!

In any case, I am eternally grateful for the part of my consciousness that decided to slack off at work, read a strange spiritual text, and hear the written whisper. Otherwise I might still be there at the office.

Great story, but what actually IS a spiritual awakening?

In all honesty I was trying to avoid this part, because trying to describe it in words is like trying to explain unicorn glitter to Darth Vader or quantum physics to a toddler. Quite challenging. The part of our consciousness that yearns to *understand* Enlightenment is not the same part that is capable of *experiencing* it. The mind wants to know what it is and have it all figured out, but in order to actually experience it, the mind needs to get out of the way.

The moment you try to define it with words, you have missed it. The first verse of the *Tao Te Ching*, the spiritual text of Taoism written by Lao Tzu, states, "The tao that can be described is not the eternal Tao. The name that can be spoken is not the eternal Name." In simpler terms, if you can explain it in words, it's not enlightenment. "Don't mistake the finger pointing to the moon, for the moon itself," warns a popular Buddhist saying. The big E can only be fully grasped through firsthand experience. It can't be understood by reading a book or hearing someone else describe their experience.

So why in Buddha's name am I writing about it? Well, words are not completely useless. The enlightened masters all say in one form or another that words are like Google Maps. Though they cannot walk the path for us, words can help show us the way, even directing us toward a faster route to go experience it for ourselves. After all, I had my first glimpse of awakening, my first real shift in consciousness, after reading an online text at the office.

Many definitions of enlightenment, from people considerably more enlightened than me, focus on defusing the destructive, chatty roommate living inside your head: your mind.

The Buddha, which literally means "the enlightened or awakened one," spoke of the mind this way:

> *To enjoy good health, to bring true happiness to one's family, to bring peace to all, one must first discipline and control one's own mind. If a man can control his mind, he can find the way to Enlightenment.*

Thousands of years after Buddha, today's illuminated Prince of Presence Eckhart Tolle takes a similar view:

> *The single most vital step on your journey toward enlightenment is this: learn to disidentify from your mind. Every time you create a gap in the stream of mind, the light of your consciousness grows stronger.*

A central aspect of awakening is realizing that you are not your thoughts. You are the awareness that is able to hear them, observe them, and let them go the moment you also realize that these thoughts are not serving you. Quite often they are actually hurting you and keeping you from seeing existence as it really is.

Indian sage Ramana Maharshi famously taught the "Who am I?" method of self-inquiry for reaching enlightenment. When a student had any thought at all that included the word "I", such as "I am happy", "I see a tree", or "I have a headache," Maharshi challenged him or her to ask, "Who is happy?" "Who is seeing the tree?" "Who has a head that aches?" Enlightenment is simply realizing that there is no "I" that is separate from the object being perceived, or identified wholly with some fleeting physical or emotional state. The separate I is an illusion.

We delude ourselves into thinking we are the main character in the movie of our life, *My Life* Starring I, Me, and Myself. But we are actually the movie *screen* the entire thing is projected onto. Everything we see, feel, and think is a projection from our own mind.

Okay, but what's really so great about enlightenment?

This isn't about meditating for eternity, learning to levitate, or performing fancy mind-reading tricks—although some of that certainly sounds cool. It's about basic human sanity and survival. The biggest threat to our collective well-being, the greatest source of pain, suffering, and destruction in the world, is the human mind. Wars are being waged by egos and mass mental delusions about "the enemy." Mass destruction to the planet is being fueled by the mind's insatiable hunger for more stuff and more profits.

LOST & FOUND

On an individual level, the mind creates more total suffering for its owner than all external forces combined. Jealousy, anger, fear, hatred, anxiety, depression. The vast majority of time, these emotional states originate in the mind and then create pain and suffering that is felt in the body.

Ever since I adopted a daily meditation practice, I have started noticing the exact moment that a negative thought in my mind creates a negative feeling in my body. It happens almost instantly, but the chain of cause-and-effect is undeniable. *Holy shit*, I observe, *here is a front row seat to my mind poisoning my body, and the energy around me, with this utterly pointless, negative thought.*

Living full-time in this unconscious, neurotic state is needless agony for yourself and everyone you interact with. Awakening out of it and seeing the world as it really is, untainted by the constant chatter and judgment of the mind, is the greatest treasure I can possibly imagine.

If you have seen *The Matrix* movies, they serve as a great, albeit disturbing, allegory for awakening. Most people go through their entire lives asleep or unconscious without realizing it. Identified completely with the constant chatter in their mind and the constantly changing emotions in their body, they are unaware that this is not the real world.

Are there different stages or levels to enlightenment?

There are no neatly defined or universally accepted levels like graduating from brown belt to black belt in karate. But spiritual teachers tend to distinguish between *conditional* enlightenment, where you get temporary glimpses of awakening and drop back into your previous sleepy state, and *permanent* enlightenment, where you remain in that state of higher consciousness.

The Buddhist monk and teacher Thich Nhat Hanh had a refreshingly foolproof take on the matter of levels:

> *Enlightenment is always there. Small enlightenment will bring great enlightenment. If you breathe in and are aware that you are alive—that you can touch the miracle of being alive—then that is a kind of enlightenment.*

Wayne Dyer held a similar uncomplicated view:

> *In my own life I know that my state of cheerfulness is a reliable gauge of my level of spiritual enlightenment at that moment.*

In other words, enlightenment is not rocket science, despite being a lofty, mystifying word. It exists right where you are in any given moment, if you can only get your mind out of the way and let yourself fully experience it.

Eckhart Tolle warns against the active striving for enlightenment, as if it were a new life level to unlock someday, if you only try hard enough.

> *You are not seeking to attain some future state. That is the fallacy of many spiritual seekers.*

LOST & FOUND

You can only be enlightened here and now, in this present moment. There is nothing superhuman to achieve, no magic quota of hours spent meditating. We have nothing more to do or to find in order to be enlightened.

I named this section Finding Enlightenment intentionally, though many spiritual teachers say that there is technically nothing to "find." We are all enlightened already, we have simply forgotten it. So becoming enlightened / awakened / present / liberated from the illusion that we are our thoughts is not a matter of finding or attaining this state but merely a matter of remembering it within ourselves. "You find God the moment you realize that you don't need to seek God," writes Tolle. To this I would say, *potato, potahto.* I agree with his point and don't want to get tangled in semantics. Enlightenment can only be found within, in this now moment, and finding it is as easy (or as difficult) as recognizing that you already have / are it. Just as finding love and finding happiness in previous sections of this book are also, at their core, states that can only fully be found within, not outside of yourself, and only in the present moment.

If this is all starting to sound a bit dry and overly serious, the next chapter will surely fix that.

20

THE FIRST STEP TO ENLIGHTENMENT

It's seriously fun

What do Neo-hippie havens like Bali, Guatemala, and Sri Lanka have in common?

Sure, you can take a very scenic and affordable yoga class in all three, sandwiched between a cacao ceremony and a Tantra workshop. But that's a surface-level similarity. I mean on a deeper, energetic level.

Over the last few years, I have spent much time in spiritual communities around the world, including the gorgeous trio listed above. I noticed something sobering: Many of my fellow soul-seekers seem to take spirituality very seriously.

It's inner *work*, after all. No one is smiling during meditation. Super-potent, serious plant medicines like ayahuasca and Bufo Alvarius (a psychedelic toad venom deemed five times more powerful than ayahuasca) are surging in popularity. There is crying and vomiting—and very little laughter.

People behave more like spiritual warriors battling their dark shadows and inner demons than as spiritual pacifists spreading love, joy and light. Healing ceremonies using kambo

LOST & FOUND

(Amazonian frog poison) literally leave you with a permanent battle scar at the site where the poison is injected into your body. A handful of my friends proudly wear this multi-circle burn scar on their upper arm and other body parts.

Kambo is called "warrior medicine." Ancient tribesmen reportedly took it before battle to make themselves feel more invincible. But today most of our battles are internal.

In a *New York Times* article, one woman credits the medicine with helping purge internalized anger from her divorce. "It was the worst experience of my life," another recalls, "and I can't wait to do it again." The article's author Alex Williams summarizes kambo's somewhat baffling appeal: "The idea is to make yourself feel horrible so that you may, after, feel wonderful."[21]

Without a doubt, confronting our unprocessed pain and traumas is a vital part of personal healing and spiritual growth. But so is leaving room for levity along the way.

The first step to enlightenment? Lighten up!

The extraterrestrial called Bashar, whose wisdom for Earthlings has been channeled by Darryl Anka for nearly forty years, has been widely quoted with saying, "The first step towards true enlightenment is to lighten up on yourself."

Bashar has traveled the planet(s) speaking to large human audiences about the importance of pursuing your passion in life. Often asked about the fastest way to reach the big E, he answers with a smile, "If you want to get enlightened, then simply lighten up!"

Keith 'The Chocolate Shaman' does a delightfully simple guided meditation that echoes Bashar's advice (the Glow meditation I referenced in Chapter 9):

"Let the smile in your heart find you. And when it does, actually smile. Let a big goofy grin spread over your face. If you're having trouble grinning because you've been taught that meditation is a serious pursuit, I'll come around and tickle you!"

Strangely enough, until Keith threatened to tickle me, the thought of smiling during meditation had never crossed my mind. I had always pictured serious monks in serious robes, seated solemnly with their eyes closed.

And yet, what do most enlightened masters have in common? A great sense of humor. They don't take spirituality or themselves too seriously.

The Dalai Lama is often asked how he can be so happy when his people have suffered so much. "I have been confronted with many difficulties throughout the course of my life, and my country is going through a critical period. But I laugh often, and my laughter is contagious. When people ask me how I find the strength to laugh now, I reply that I am a professional laugher."[22]

Spiritual author Ram Dass gave us comedic gems like "Your problem is you're too busy holding on to your unworthiness," and "If you think you're enlightened, go spend a week with your family."

Then there's Matt Kahn, who describes himself as a spiritual teacher and highly attuned, empathic, intuitive healer. That's a bit of a mouthful, so I describe him to my friends as a spiritual comedian.

Kahn's books, YouTube videos, and global "soul gatherings" have attracted millions of followers. His transmissions have me laughing out loud in between my mind being blown and my inner guru nodding along. (I challenge you to get through his free talk on Twin Flames and Soulmates[23] without cracking up.)

Similarly, when I read the wisdom of self-help legends like Wayne Dyer and the modern musings of Mark Manson, their ideas are impactful precisely because they use humor to explain concepts that would otherwise sound trite, complicated or preachy.

Even Eckhart Tolle, the literary heavyweight behind *The Power of Now*, has been known to crack some jokes about awakening. "I have lived with several Zen Masters—all of them cats."

※

Years ago I met a fellow traveler while living in Guatemala. We bonded over our similar life paths. She, too, had recently quit her demanding job in New York City to travel the world. She, too, would end up teaching yoga. She eventually settled in Cambodia and began teaching "Joyshops" instead of workshops. Lately, I have also seen "Playshops" being advertised on community events boards for various trainings in the realm of personal growth.

Okay, it's a bit cutesy, this play on words. But it's also nice to be reminded that all this spiritual stuff, all this working on ourselves designed to ultimately bring more joy and love into our lives, doesn't have to feel so much like *work*.

In all honesty I am writing these words as much for myself as for others. I still need the reminder to lighten up in pursuit of enlightenment. At times it does feel like work. Like when my alarm goes off at 6:30 AM every morning to go meditate in a group. Will spiritual awakening feel as glorious as an extra hour of human sleeping? I can't help wonder.

Or when my ego tricks me into comparing my spiritual progress with that of others. My partner has been meditating for over 20 years and can go impressively long stretches of time without having a single thought. Relatively speaking, I am still on training wheels.

But the number and size of my wheels is nobody else's business. Is it?

When did spirituality become a competitive sport?
One of the most hippie towns I have ever encountered—at least based on the prevalence of man-buns and mandala tattoos—is the lakeside Mayan village San Marcos La Laguna (my unexpected new home).

"In San Marcos, people compete for who can give the longest hug," an ex-pat yoga teacher with long dreads explained when I first arrived. She was only half-joking.

I initially stayed in San Marcos for a few months, doing all the competitive hugging and ecstatic dancing I could handle. Somewhere along the way I realized that there's a big difference between pursuing spiritual awakening to dissolve the ego versus to feed it. Sometimes the difference is subtle: for example, a seemingly advanced meditator who secretly looks down on non-meditators is likely meditating to boost his spiritual ego and feel superior.

Other times the difference is flaming obvious: there are actual yoga *competitions* being held around the world today. Yogis compete against each other on how well they perform advanced physical asanas (postures). Competitive yoga is gaining popularity and one day hopes to be an official Olympic sport. A personal spiritual practice has mutated into a public spectacle. I can't quite wrap my head around it. Though I *can* wrap my legs around my head, so perhaps I should consider competing.

Western yoga has veered so far from its Eastern roots as a moving meditation that we might as well call it something else. Noga? Sanskrit Stretching? Gymnastics for Instagram? There is nothing inherently wrong with an activity that promotes physical and mental flexibility. But to award trophies for something called yoga would be like forming a competitive surgery league for ER doctors. Sure, you technically could, but you would be missing the entire point of why yoga and emergency rooms exist.

The Yoga Olympics makes me uncomfortable for obvious reasons, but most spiritual practices are less black and white. I am still searching for the line between healthy spiritual work and unhealthy spiritual extremes.

There are 3-day meditation retreats and 30-day meditation retreats. Actually, there are ones triple that length, if you lean toward extremes. I have done a 5-day silent retreat and considered the popular 10-day Vipassana. But I can't for the silent life of me imagine what I would do with 90 days of voluntary solitary confinement. It sounds like escaping from society, which can certainly be tempting. But in the words of Dutch priest Henri Nouwen, "The spiritual life does not remove us from the world but leads us deeper into it."

During my first stint living in San Marcos, I met a young woman who had just completed forty days of silence at a nearby meditation center. I had recently finished my very first silent retreat (five days) and felt genuinely proud of myself—it had not been easy. Stunned to learn that regular Westerners my age were capable of shutting up for forty days, I stared at this woman in awe and peppered her with questions. Was it hard? How was she feeling now? She stared back at me like a sedated deer in headlights. Interacting with people was simply too much after all that silence. I sincerely hope she gained some lasting healing and positive changes from the experience, rather than finding it harder to integrate back into normal life, with all its noises and triggers.

Everyone is on their own beautiful path of healing and awakening. Yet it's hard not to get sucked into the spiritual milestones we are supposed to hit along the way, and even harder not to forget that we are allowed to have fun along the way. Beyond sobering silent retreats, there are intensive breathwork treatments, womb reactivations, sacred sound bath ceremonies, and weeklong water fasts "with high vibrational alkalized Kangen water." I actually drank this water for a few days once but made the rookie mistake of pairing it with food.

And if you haven't done ayahuasca yet, are you even spiritual?

Spiritual AF, to be exact

JP Sears has long red hair, chiseled abs, and a penchant for wearing yoga tights objectively too tight.

His internet-famous guides, like "How To Be Ultra-Spiritual" are as funny as they are accurate in their depiction of self-described spiritual people today. With tips like *Use the word Namaste often* and *Do copious amounts of yoga*, it's funny precisely because it's true.

JP has millions of followers across social media platforms, a book, a touring comedy show, and an online store where you can buy "Woke AF" tees and "Spiritual As Hell" hoodies. He is most popular with the very people he makes fun of—the modern spiritual class of yogis, meditators, and people who use the word energy constantly.

On YouTube he states, "Perhaps our ability to laugh at ourselves and not take ourselves too seriously is what increases our spiritual growth."

You may not agree with everything he says, but his satirical approach is a refreshing antidote to the purely serious side of spirituality. Sears also says, "Humor and seriousness are perhaps two important keys that open the doors of our heart and soul. If we have one and not the other, we're at least half locked out of our own self."

On a subconscious level, I wonder if we are afraid to let ourselves have too much fun on the spiritual path because deep down we equate enlightenment with suffering and disciplined, hard work. There's no such thing as a free lunch, right?

How much suffering is necessary before awakening?
William Sutcliffe's *Are You Experienced?* is a hilarious tale about the absurdities of the modern spiritual quest—specifically when relatively affluent youth from Western countries travel to less cushy locales like India to find themselves.

The protagonist, a British backpacker who follows his crush to India, observes, "Everyone seemed to have big ideas about how they had to find themselves, whatever that meant, through some journey to a poverty-stricken flea-pit half-way up a malaria-infested mountain on the other side of the planet. There was a general belief that a long and unpleasant holiday was of crucial importance to one's development as a human being."[24]

But *does* there have to be suffering in order to attain spiritual enlightenment? Eckhart Tolle says, "Suffering is necessary until you realize that it is unnecessary." This is annoyingly cryptic if you happen to be suffering, and amusingly obvious if you are not. The power to stop suffering and shift our consciousness into enlightenment is fully in our hands, but only if we realize and acknowledge this power (rather than giving it away to other people or external situations). Tolle further advises, "In some rare cases, this shift in consciousness happens dramatically and radically, once and for all. When it does, it usually comes about through total surrender in the midst of intense suffering. Most people, however, have to work at it."

Many spiritual teachers echo this. Pain and suffering can drastically accelerate the awakening process if the person is able to find presence and surrender in the midst of it or in the aftermath of a traumatic event. If instead the person remains unconscious, feeding the pain and identifying firmly as a victim, the suffering will only continue.

Through our own personal blend of traumas and pain accumulated throughout our lives, most of us will have to work at awakening. It can be a slow, gradual process as we learn from our life's struggles. I used to see my personal struggles with anxiety and loneliness as the universe being against me and as proof of me being undeserving of happiness and love. When I started on the spiritual path, I realized that those struggles were (and continue to be) blessed opportunities to grow and awaken more deeply and permanently.

In one of my lowest moments, I had an anxiety attack toward the end of an exceptionally stressful 80-hour workweek. As I sat alone in a Chicago hotel room on the eve of a big client presentation, I found myself crying and laughing at the same time. Even in the midst of my pain and exhaustion, some part of me could sense the absurdity of it all. Here I was in a plush hotel bathrobe, stress-eating every chocolate from the minibar, spilling tears on my peanut M&Ms. There was no real imminent problem in sight, only the one I had created in my mind.

The sadness subsided and left me with a lasting insight. When I look at the overwhelming majority of my life, one theme predominates: I am so lucky. I have been blessed with a supportive family, true friends, years of travel adventures, and (eventually) a loving partner. Sure, there have been obstacles and pain, both physical and emotional. But most of my suffering has come from inside my own head. From wanting or expecting life to be different in some way. From believing that my happiness lies outside of myself.

> *Suffering just means you're having a bad dream. Happiness means you're having a good dream. Enlightenment means getting out of the dream altogether.* —Jed McKenna

Until I manage to get out of the dream and awaken fully, I would strongly prefer to have more good dreams than bad dreams. A little more laughter and joy than tears and sadness.

The first step to enlightenment is to lighten up. And until enlightenment, lightening up is its own reward.

21

THE PERKS OF DATING A MEDITATION TEACHER

I'm ready to spill some of his spiritual secrets

When my partner Herb was a young boy growing up in Montana, he started reading meditation books. For fun. His own family thought it was strange.

At 18 he began teaching meditation at a local college and has since taught around the world.

If our meditation streaks were people, his would be legally allowed to buy alcohol. Mine would be learning how to roll over on its tummy.

The point here is not that length matters. In fact, Herb freely admits he "felt like an idiot" when he finally realized the secrets below after many years of meditating. I bring you his wisdom for two reasons:

1. To rapidly accelerate your own meditation practice—or at least save you from ditching it out of boredom or frustration

2. To provide a little teaser trailer for the book that Herb is currently writing himself. With his permission, I

share a snippet of his teachings so that they may reach an even wider audience.

I may be relatively new to daily meditation, but I'm no stranger to spiritual communities and perspectives. I have studied dozens of texts, completed silent retreats, and attempted various meditation techniques over the years. The concepts my partner teaches seem both stupid-simple and slightly counter-intuitive. But more importantly, they seem to actually work.

Without further ado, here are some of Herb's favorite meditation myth-busters and general tips gleaned from 20-plus years of experiential wisdom.

Don't sit in a quiet place

This might sound crazy, but try meditating in a place with noise and distractions on purpose. Cars passing, dogs barking, people talking. These annoying acoustics are not actually obstacles to meditation. They are accelerants to your meditation practice.

It is relatively easy to slip into a calm, relaxed state when you have no external stimuli. Meditating at a secluded silent retreat center for a week can help you go deeper and access higher states of consciousness. But then you leave the retreat and return to your normal life. Unless you live in a Tibetan monastery, your normal life is probably the opposite of secluded and peaceful.

Only meditating in quiet places with no distractions would be like going to the gym every day and doing the bicep-curl arm motion without ever actually picking up the weights. Never challenging your meditation workout will keep your practice on training wheels.

Herb used to teach in a spiritual community in Guatemala with self-proclaimed advanced meditators. He would guide them into a peaceful state and then poke students at random with a wooden "WTF stick". It was usually met with a pair of annoyed-to-be-opened eyes and a facial expression that read *Dude, WTF?*

If you are getting thrown off balance by a little nudge during meditation, how are you going to react when there's a real trigger in your daily life? When your boss yells or someone cuts you off in traffic? When someone breaks your heart?

Meditation should prepare you for life, not simply for stillness.

Ask yourself if you have a meditation practice or a thinking practice

You might look like a Zen monk to the outside observer, calmly sitting with your eyes closed, fingers pressed into a mudra. But if you are lost in your thoughts, it is literally the opposite of meditating.

Herb instructs students to ask themselves one crucial question at the end of a meditation: Did I really just meditate, or simply sit quietly and think for 30 minutes?

Many people spend years assuming they are meditating, when really they are thinking with their eyes closed. It's perfectly okay if the answer to this question is sometimes "Yep, Thoughts City; Population: Me." Especially when starting out. Our brains are so firmly wired into the infinite loop of mental chatter that the idea of silencing thoughts sounds impossible without the aid of a lobotomy.

Initially there might be no space between your thoughts. *I can't wait for breakfastMy nose itchesI hate meditatingWhy didn't I wear my looser pantsHey whatever happened to those blue pants I bought ten years agoDid I mention I hate meditating?*

Then you will start to notice little gaps in between the thoughts. Perhaps a few seconds of silence until the next thought arrives. Gradually those spaces will widen. One day you will catch yourself thinking, *Sweet Buddha! I just went a whole minute without thinkin—aw crap, now I'm thinking again.*

Eventually something crazy will happen...

One day your thoughts will completely disappear

Herb's default demeanor is calm and relaxed, like you might expect from a lifelong meditator. But if you want to see him riled up, tell him you heard a so-called meditation expert say that *thoughts will always arise*.

It's a HUGE meditation myth that thoughts will always keep coming and going. Anyone teaching you this simply has not gone deep enough in their own practice.

LOST & FOUND

Herb regularly reports spending lengthy stretches of time with a blissfully thought-less mind. He's not gloating (well, maybe a little). He wants others to personally experience this mystical level of presence.

He distinguishes an intermediate meditator from a beginner as such: the former can go five whole minutes without a single thought. No bubbling up of a thought. No fragments. Zilch. Nada. Blankety-blank.

Once or twice I have lasted about 30 seconds sans thinking and felt like levitation was mere moments away. One hundred times I have sat there and cursed myself for being a crappy meditator and felt crappy in general. Which brings us to the next secret.

It's not always supposed to feel good

There's a silly belief that if you're doing meditation right, it should make you feel only peace, joy and love. More broadly we assume that being spiritual means sunshine and unicorn glitter will shoot out of your...aura. So if unspiritual sensations like sadness or anger arise during meditation, we tend to push them back down. *Nope, I don't want to feel THAT.*

Yet that's exactly what we should allow ourselves to feel in that moment if we want to finally release that pain. "The cure for pain is in the pain," said Rumi. When you are truly meditating, being present with whatever arises for you in the moment instead of lost in a mental story, negative emotions and repressed traumas start to bubble up.

If a child is crying, and his father yells, "Shut up! Big boys don't cry"—that's the energy you are sending yourself if you push negative feelings back down. Push those feelings down enough times and they even begin to show up as physical pain in the body.

It's not fun to feel pain. And culturally we have bought into this total hogwash that the sign of spiritual growth and personal progress is feeling happy all the time. The REAL sign of progress is allowing whatever arises, not trying to bypass it, judge it or hate it. Can you love the part of yourself that is hurting right now? That is how pain gets transmuted and released.

Avoiding unpleasant feelings and not doing your inner work is called spiritual bypassing. It's one of Herb's favorite topics to discuss in his classes and during our dinner dates. I know. I'm a lucky gal.

Don't forget to open your eyes

"Meditating with your eyes closed is the beginner practice," Herb says. "The advanced practice begins when you open them."

The real practice is going about your normal day in the same state of presence and thought-free awareness as when you sit with your eyes closed. Being able to finally see the world without the labels and judgments your mind puts on everything.

Try doing the most mundane activities without having thoughts. Can you simply be present and watch yourself tie your shoes or wash the dishes? Can you have a conversation with someone and truly *listen* to them with a blank mind? Can you hold space instead of running a mental commentary on what the other person is saying, or planning out what you are going to say next?

Then there is mindfulness, the most misunderstood open-eye meditation practice today. You see people being 'mindful' by strolling in slow motion through a forest. They confuse hyper-focus with true present awareness. You can be mindful at a dead sprint. It has nothing to do with going slow. Can you look at the trees without your mind labeling them as "trees" or even as "green"? Can you simply SEE without the filter of thought?

Don't mistake meditation's side effects for its purpose

Herb likes to start class by asking people why they meditate, or why they want to start. The common answers roll in. To feel more peaceful, relaxed, happy. To have more clarity and focus. To sleep better.

He counters that these are all wonderful *side effects* of meditation. They are not the main reason to do it.

The true purpose of meditation has many names but the same experience. Awakening. Enlightenment. Satori. Nirvana. Illumination. Freedom from suffering. Waking up from unconsciousness. From the illusion that you are your thoughts, or that anything exists except the present moment.

Meditation comes with obstacles. Your body and mind will try to distract you. But the payoff for practice and persistence is immeasurable.

The fastest path to awakening is not what you think

ALLA POLSKY

Who would you guess is likely to reach enlightenment faster—a monk meditating in solitude in a cave for twenty years, or a person in a romantic relationship living a relatively normal life and meditating sporadically?

Relationships aren't easy. The person who knows you best also knows how to push your buttons better than anyone. But when you get upset, feel angry or hurt—all these emotional triggers are actually spiritual treasures. They are love in disguise, showing you exactly where YOU need to work on yourself. They are a giant blinking arrow to the path of dissolving your ego faster than that monk in a cave. He has chosen a loin-clothed life that is relatively free of triggers. Free of the spiritual accelerants that come with getting close to people, with baring your heart and soul to another.

Herb and I have an amusing agreement to call each other out when we have "gone unconscious."

Honey, your ego is flaring. Are you being present?
I'm not sure. Presently I want to punch you.

This is perhaps the biggest perk of dating a meditation teacher. We constantly teach each other about ourselves. We point out each other's blind spots in pursuit of accelerating personal and spiritual growth. It feels silly and annoying and amazing all at once.

I told Herb that I intended to name this chapter "Spiritual Sh*t My Boyfriend Says." His eyes rolled upward, either out of exasperation or in a blissful gaze at his third eye.

Probably the latter. With triggers flying back and forth, I can't help but wonder which of us will awaken first.

22

MY DEAD GRANDMA HELPS ME LUCID DREAM

And yours can, too!

I am sitting in my parents' living room, holding my grandmother's hand. My mother and sister are there, too. Suddenly a clear knowing hits me: My grandmother died earlier this year. So unless I found a working time machine, this experience can't be real.

I must be having a dream, I think to myself.

If there was any shred of doubt left in my mind about whether this was, in fact, a dream, I look down at my grandma's hand—the one I am still holding. It has three fingers.

Yep. Definitely a dream. Living Grandma had five fingers.

The instant grief I feel upon remembering that she is still dead is joined by the indescribable thrill of knowing that I am having the first lucid dream of my life.

Be cool, I tell myself. *Don't get overly excited, or you will wake yourself up.*

I had been doing special exercises for months in my waking hours to help me awaken within my dreams. None of them had worked—until Grandma showed up.

ALLA POLSKY

What is a lucid dream, exactly?

The concept of lucid dreaming first entered my consciousness via Hollywood. I was enthralled by the movie *Inception* starring Leonardo DiCaprio. By its notion of a shared dream world and all the things that became possible in a dream state if you only knew that you were sleeping.

Movies sell drama and imagination, not accuracy, so undoubtedly some creative liberties were taken with the logistical mechanics of lucid dreaming. But once I learned more about its off-screen realities and possibilities, the true wonders of lucid dreaming eclipsed anything that a screenwriter could dream up.

A lucid dream occurs when the dreamer becomes aware that they are dreaming. This conscious awareness that you are in the middle of a dream is the first stage of lucid dreaming.

The first few times it happens, dreamers tend to wake themselves up out of excitement, or they slip back into non-lucid dreaming. But with practice, one is able to stay lucid in the dream for longer and start to control the dream itself.

When you learn to take control, the natural inclination is to live out your fantasies in the dream state. Fly around like Superman. Get frisky with a hot celebrity or someone you desire in real life. Bend reality to your will in ways only limited by your own imagination.

But if you want to really go for a wild ride in the dream world, *sit down to meditate*. No, seriously.

Why would I want to meditate when I could fly around?

LOST & FOUND

In his book *Dreaming Yourself Awake*, Alan Wallace takes the experience of lucid dreaming far beyond entertainment. Lucid dreaming is not only a powerful research-backed tool to boost creativity and solve your waking-world problems from the comfort of your pillow. It's also an ancient tool for spiritual awakening.

For thousands of years, Tibetan Buddhists have been using advanced lucid dreaming techniques in both their dreaming and waking states in order to attain the ultimate Awakening. Called Dream Yoga, it bridges the lucidity in our dreams with the ability to become more lucid, or aware, in our daily waking life.

In other words, lucid dreaming gives way to lucid living. Waking up out of the illusion that we are all separate, non-spiritual beings. Waking up to the realization that the world our consciousness creates while we sleep is no more or less 'real' than the reality we perceive when we are awake. It is all a dream. Writer Jed McKenna's quote bears repeating:

> *Suffering just means you're having a bad dream.*
> *Happiness means you're having a good dream.*
> *Enlightenment means getting out of the dream altogether.*

In my very first lucid dream, I let go of my grandma's three-fingered hand and immediately sat down to meditate. Herb had recommended this course of action, and I was insatiably curious to see where it led.

ALLA POLSKY

My lucid meditation lasted only a few moments. I was too excited to have finally awakened within a dream. My imagined family members kept on talking and distracting me. But I could already sense the powerful potential of meditating inside of a dream, of exploring deeper states of my consciousness. I could not wait to try again.

Nearly a month passes until my second lucid dream. It's Grandma to the rescue again. I am hanging out with her and my mom, and again I realize in an instant that this must be a dream.

Grandma is dead, so this cannot be real.

Except this time I share the realization out loud in my dream. My mom hears the rude awakening that her mother is actually dead, and she starts to cry. Her tears slip me back into the non-lucid dream state. It's almost as if I decide to maintain the illusion for her sake. To spare my mother from extra grief by pretending that the dream is real, that her own mother is still alive.

When I awake, I realize that my own subconscious was doing imagined favors at the expense of my own spiritual expansion. I wonder why I chose to hold myself back.

How do you learn to lucid dream?

You are looking for glitches in the matrix. Little discrepancies between your waking world and your dream world. The appearance of deceased loved ones is a common one. So is the appearance of famous people. (Herb meditated with Jesus in one lucid dream and spoke with Yoda in another.) Train your consciousness to continually ask yourself, "Is this person actually in my life today?"

Although my grandma seems to be the most palpable discrepancy for me, I did have one lucid dream thanks to my living cat Greta. She had gotten herself tangled up in a rope from some camping gear. As I untangled and loosened the rope from her fluffy neck and chest, she replied in perfect English—with a British accent, no less. "Oh my, thank you for getting me out of that predicament! It was getting hard to breathe!"

I instantly said to myself, "Waaait a minute. Greta is a cat. She does not, to my knowledge, have the ability to speak English. This must be a dream!" We then had a lively conversation. I wasn't going to waste the opportunity to converse with my cat beyond the usual purrs and meows.

Another popular lucid dreaming technique is to find an anchor in your waking life. Something that you do many times throughout the day, like walking through a doorway or checking your phone. Every time you do this activity, ask yourself, "Am I awake right now or am I dreaming?" Eventually, the answer will be, "Holy crap, I'm dreaming!"

Look for clues that something is off. Commonly in dreams, the digits on a clock will change each time you look at them. Same with the words in a book. Look away, and look back. They will have morphed into something else.

Counting fingers is also popular. Whether on your own hand or someone else's, as I did with my grandma. The chances are, there will not be five fingers if you are dreaming.

A technique that has worked for several friends is the palm touch. Throughout the day, look at the palm of your hand (always the same hand) and ask yourself, "Am I awake?" as you try to push your other hand's index finger through the palm. Have the intention of actually pushing it through. Do this fifty times a day. Eventually, the palm touch will infiltrate one of your dreams. Your finger will go through the palm, making you realize that you are dreaming.

Several months pass by without a single lucid dream, despite my grandmother appearing in a few regular dreams. I have almost given up on my dream of lucidity when something peculiar happens. I am in an airport with my entire family, grandma included. Worried that we will be late for our flight if we don't start walking toward the departure gate, I urge the family to get a head start while I run to the bathroom. There is a long line, and now I am the one who is late. Anxiously weaving through crowds to catch up to them, an idea forms: this would be so much faster *if I could fly.* To my surprise, I instantly lift off the ground and find myself able to fly through the terminal.

In that moment I realize I am dreaming (airplanes can fly, humans not so much). I lose interest in catching up with my imagined family and allow myself to enjoy the lucid flight. I do forward rolls and backward rolls and other tricks in the air, laughing like a kid. I clear the crowds with my mind in order to have more space to play. The experience feels every bit as vivid and *real* as real life, even though I am fully aware that this is a dream. Eventually I remember to try meditating. I gently float back down to the ground and sit in a lotus posture. Other travelers immediately stop by to distract me. A former college roommate randomly shows up and peppers me with questions. The meditation fails but I awake from the dream feeling successful, though also wondering why my own subconscious tried to distract me from meditating.

Since that airport dream, I have had several more involving flying but none involving my grandma. Each time I slipped back into non-lucid dreaming before I could really start to play with my environment and change the dream at will. There is no shortage of incentives to master this advanced stage of lucid dreaming: if I can learn to stabilize my lucid dreams and take conscious control of what happens in them, then I could summon my grandma at will instead of waiting for her to appear. I could also meditate for hours without my legs falling asleep, and make pesky distractions disappear.

I suspect that meditating in a dream state might unlock the mysteries of higher consciousness and accelerate my spiritual awakening. What could be better than that? I can only think of one thing: hanging out with my grandma and my cat, discussing the mysteries of life in a British accent.

23

My Living Boyfriend Hypnotizes Me

It's nothing like what you see on TV

There are probably more misconceptions about hypnosis than there are neurons in the brain. I blindly believed all of them until I began dating Herb and experienced the fascinating state of being hypnotized for myself.

First, the misconceptions

Contrary to popular belief, hypnosis is not mind control. Quite the opposite, actually. It aims to give *you* more control over your own mind and body. More power from within to make the positive life changes you have struggled to achieve thus far. Changes like quitting a bad habit (smoking, procrastinating), creating more positive habits (exercising, eating healthy), overcoming a debilitating fear (flying, public speaking), or releasing unconscious patterns that are making you sabotage your relationships or career success.

If the hypnotist tries to plant a suggestion in your mind that does not align with your own personal values, belief system, or highest good, you will often automatically come out of the hypnotic state. "At the end of this session, you will have an overwhelming desire to give me ten thousand dollars—It just doesn't work like that," Herb explains. It is actually very difficult to "brainwash" someone into hurting another person, for instance, unless they already deeply want to do that thing.

The entertainment industry is not exactly known for its accurate portrayal of professions. Hypnosis as brainwashing and mind control, while complete fiction, gets better ratings than hypnosis as it really is: a highly effective way to bypass the conscious thinking mind, which only controls about 5% of your behaviors and beliefs. Hypnosis speaks directly to your unconscious mind, the part of you that runs largely on autopilot without your conscious awareness. This is where the vast majority of your true beliefs, motivations, fears, and traumas actually reside. It's why talk therapy doesn't always work—it speaks to your conscious mind. This rational part of you may genuinely want to make positive changes, but deep in the subconscious, your true control center is resisting or vetoing those changes.

Hypnotherapy, or the use of hypnosis for therapeutic purposes, goes straight for the control center. And it's nothing like the stage hypnosis used for comedic entertainment. Sure, you could hypnotize someone to bark like a dog or momentarily forget the number eight. Cheap tricks for cheap laughs. Or you could use hypnosis to radically improve someone's life. Help them make lasting changes and heal unconscious traumas (as Chapter 17 showed, most of us have some).

I have seen people float out of Herb's office after a hypnotherapy session as if existing in a new dimension of reality. Many of them shared the results with me: clarity toward their life purpose, years of emotional blockages cleared, more confidence in career and relationships, no more panic attacks, zero urge to touch a cigarette again (even months later).

I am not trying to sell you on hypnosis. When the hypnotherapist is talented, compassionate, and non-shady, hypnosis sells itself. Herb gets booked out a month in advance for private sessions and has to turn people away because his schedule is full. I wish I could hypnotize him to work less, but alas, his subconscious would reject the suggestion. Helping people is his life's calling.

Another huge misconception is that some people cannot be hypnotized. Everyone can, as long as they approach the experience willingly and the therapist is skilled enough to adjust techniques based on the client's response. Herb has worked with hundreds of people and every single one was able to access a hypnotic state.

What is this state, exactly? It's a naturally occurring state of deeper consciousness that is activated when a person's mind is brought to the edge of sleep. Unlike in actual sleep, in hypnosis your mind is still awake, fully aware of what's happening and where you are. With your body feeling completely relaxed in a safe, comfortable environment, your subconscious mind becomes more open to suggestions and experiences that will help transform your life.

My own experience

One of the perks of dating a clinical hypnotherapist is, of course, free sessions (when his busy schedule allows). I am not a total freeloader and always insist on paying him with kisses and nice dinners. In my twenty or so sessions with Hypnotic Herb (a working nickname), we have tackled everything from sleeping better to managing anxiety and stress to clearing writer's block to releasing childhood traumas I didn't even know I had.

One session in particular stood out: my very first past-life regression. This means that while in a state of deep hypnosis—still fully awake and able to speak—my subconscious recalled several specific past lives I have previously lived.

I realize this sounds nuts if you personally do not believe our souls reincarnate to live in other bodies and other times throughout history. I wasn't sure if I fully believed it in the literal sense, but I was open to exploring this alternate state of my consciousness. Okay, I wasn't merely open to it. I was curious as hell.

Herb was quick to remind me that past life regressions are not to be used for entertainment. There should be a meaningful reason your subconscious is being asked to bring forth a particular past life into your conscious awareness. Usually that reason is to help you heal, process, or understand something better in your current life. (Sometimes people in hypnosis will spontaneously recall past lives without being asked to do so, again most likely to help heal or better understand their current life.)

Herb offers to record our session because even though I will be fully conscious and answering his questions for an hour, I may not remember much of the conversation when I come out of hypnosis. This is quite common. Sometimes people go into the deepest state of hypnosis, called a somnambulist state, and when they come out they will say, "Oh, sorry, I think I fell asleep." In reality they were having a completely coherent conversation with Herb the whole time but simply have no memory of it.

I consent to having my session recorded in case I don't remember all of it—and I'm glad I did, because now I can share excerpts from the actual recording.

The first life I recalled was seemingly to get my bearings and get the hang of this strange experience. Herb asked specific questions about who and where I was, and I responded with surprising ease.

My name was Simon (I giggled out loud upon realizing that I was in a man's body), the year was 1090 somewhere in Europe, and I felt peaceful as I walked barefoot through a field near my village.

The next life got more interesting.

I am ten years old, an orphan girl on a large ship bound for the New World. My name is Beth, I hear myself say without any hesitation. I am dressed in rags, the only child on this voyage mainly full of religious missionaries. I sense that we are from Europe, going to "civilize" the native people in the New World and convert them to Christianity. The missionaries have brought me along because I have no family, no place to be, and I can speak more than one language, perhaps be useful as a translator. That's the cover story, at least. The real reason is that I appear to have a strange gift the missionaries know about. My hands can sense when danger is near.

LOST & FOUND

It's a bodily sensation I have experienced in my current lifetime. As little Alla back in Belarus, my hands would suddenly feel dense and heavy, like I was carrying invisible weights, or my hands themselves became the weights. It felt confusing, scary, and powerful at the same time. Sensing that this wasn't exactly normal, I kept my Incredible Hulk hands to myself. As I got older, the mysterious sensation mostly disappeared except for seemingly random recurrences every five or ten years. Now I feel it again both as Alla under hypnosis, and as little Beth on a boat in the 17th century. Until now it had never occurred to me to link the physical sensation to feeling danger.

We are approaching land. I can feel the fear of the missionaries—many had no choice about this voyage into the unknown—but I myself am excited. The New World means curious new people and adventures. There is nothing left for me across the sea. The native people appear hostile at first, but they, too, are scared of us. Soon they see we mean no harm. The heaviness in my hands dissipates along with the fear on both sides.

I fast-forward in this lifetime to the age of 18. I am a young woman who has made this new land her home. I live among the native people and the few European missionaries who stayed. I anxiously await the return of my husband—he is off on a hunt, and nothing more dangerous, I hope. When he returns, I describe him as having long, black hair and the same eyes as Herb. They don't simply resemble Herb's golden brown eyes, they *are* his eyes. It would not surprise me if we have been partners in other lifetimes. Our connection in this one feels so strong, so familiar.

I describe this lifetime as rather peaceful and harmonious on the whole and express my desire to move on to another one. I have seen and understood what I needed: the source of the strange sensation in my hands, my romantic history with Native American Herb, my crossing the Atlantic in another lifetime, leaving Europe for America as a child again in this life as well.

The third and final life I recall in this session steals the show. (For clarity Herb's voice appears in *italics* and mine in regular type.)

When you scan your body, what do you notice?
I'm old. (I laugh out loud). I am lying indoors. I'm a very old man. I get the sense that I am on my deathbed.

Any sense of how old you are?
Old for the times. In my sixties at least. I am very skinny. I can see my bones.

Any sense of where you are?
I'm in a city. It feels like a French medieval town starting with a D. The year is 1530-something. 1533.

Is anyone else in the room with you?
I get a sense of family members. It's nighttime and they are asleep nearby.

LOST & FOUND

Why this particular moment? Why did you arrive in this life?
I feel like I'm actually about to die soon, about to leave this body.

Would you like to experience the transition process of death?
Yes.

What are you experiencing?
A bit of sadness and fear. Leaving my family and knowing they are going to be sad. Wanting to believe that this isn't the end, but also fearing the unknown, not being sure if there is an afterlife.

What happens when you move forward a little bit more?
I get déjà vu, actually. Like I've done this before.

This death process?
Yeah.

How are you experiencing it? What's going on in the body?
It feels like a lightness. Zero pain. I see white. It's not a white light, just a white void. I feel this pressure in my left temple, I actually feel it quite often in this life, especially during meditation.

What is this showing you?
It's a very familiar sensation. Maybe that explains part of the déjà vu. It's like a link between my body and my consciousness. It partly does live in the brain, I'm not sure why the left

side. It feels like it's the last part of me that I feel in the body before I let go of that body. I can't feel the rest of having a body anymore.

Moving forward in time, what happens then?
The pressure in my left temple goes away. What I see or sense is outer space. Stars. It's almost as if every star is a soul. I'm looking out at them but I also am one. This feels familiar, too. I'm not like, "Holy shit, look at all these stars!" I've been here before. It's almost like a homecoming.

How does the reception feel from these other stars, these other souls?
Some feel like they're very inward. They are going through their own thing right now. But some of them twinkle brighter than others. They seem closer and more familiar to me.

Are there any you need to connect with in this place?
There is one. It feels like one that was a child of mine in a lifetime, but now that we're not in our bodies, it's more of an acknowledgment. "Hey, nice to see you again."

How does that feel?
It feels—I can't quite put an emotion around it. Because in this state, emotions don't feel the same. I can say, kind of happy, but there's a detachment to emotions. So it's more like, "Hey, I know that one." It's not good or bad. It's an acknowledgment. "I see you."

LOST & FOUND

Now if it feels right to you, bringing in your higher consciousness that has a deeper overview and understanding. And if it's okay with you, I'd like to speak directly to that part of you, your higher self.
Okay, cool.

What do you have to teach Alla? Why are you showing her all this, having her experience this?
It's a reminder not to take it all so seriously. This particular lifetime she's taking VERY seriously.

What lessons can help her on this current path in this lifetime?
Definitely lighten up. And there's a much larger purpose. To help all these other souls awaken and realize not to take everything so seriously as well.

How can she do both of these things?
(Laughs) She's not gonna like it. The first thing that came to mind is "Write more."

Why does she have this resistance, not like this idea of writing more?
She just doesn't enjoy the process. It drains her.

What advice would you give her?
That it really will help people. Suck it up. It will get easier. Treat the act of writing as a fun thing. Try to make yourself

laugh while doing it. A service for others and something for yourself, too.

Anything particular she should be writing about?
She used to think it should be travel, but it's really more spirituality, relationships. The things we talk about in the hostel.

Anything beyond writing that she should know to help her along the way?
(Laughs again) I think she knows, but stop eating cheese. Or stop eating SO much cheese.

Is there anything else that Alla needs to know?
Stop being so damn hard on yourself. Keep meditating, it will get easier. Follow your instinct. Reconnect with nature, water especially. And the best is yet to come. There's going to be a lot happening in the next few years. She won't have to be patient for too much longer.
(There is a moment of silence before my higher self adds one last piece of wisdom.) She is right where she's supposed to be and right on schedule. She's not late for anything. It's important for her to know that. She is exactly right on time.

Apparently my higher self is aware that I have stressful dreams almost every night about feeling late or rushed. The scenario changes in each dream—I am stress-packing and late to catch a flight or late to meet a friend—but the underlying anxiety is the same each time.

LOST & FOUND

Whether all of these lifetimes literally took place, or my consciousness was simply trying to teach me important lessons using my imagination, I will never know. But either way I got the lessons.

I heard loud and clear that writing is an inescapable part of my purpose—it's time to stop resisting and playing small. I saw that death is not something to be feared. It's a natural part of life, and there is at least the possibility that we really have lived countless lifetimes in different bodies and eras. It's how our souls learned the hard lessons and prepared our consciousness to be ready for awakening in this lifetime.

Reincarnation is not a new or even provocative idea in many cultures and among history's greatest minds. Plato and Socrates openly believed in reincarnation, as did Benjamin Franklin and Henry Ford. The 13th century Persian poet, scholar, and mystic Rumi said:

> *This place is a dream. Only a sleeper considers it real. Then death comes like dawn, and you wake up laughing at what you thought was your grief.*

There it is again, the reminder not to take it all so seriously. Whether you connect to your higher self by closing your eyes and quieting the mind, or by looking up at the stars, or something else entirely, I honor that divine part of you that knows and remembers who you are: eternal, infinite, awake.

Oh, and it probably wouldn't hurt to eat a little less cheese.

SECRET BONUS CHAPTER

An encore and a eulogy you didn't know you needed

24

TIMELESS WISDOM FROM MY BABUSHKA

My grandmother gave unsolicited advice for 85 years. Here are the highlights.

In early 2021 my Babushka (Grandma in Russian) died from Covid. She was the center of gravity for our entire family. Its very soul.

Babushka was both highly sensitive and fiercely tough. A good hug could make her cry. And yet she was as strong as Soviet steel. Surviving war, illness, persecution. Nothing in this world frightened her except the possibility of 1) ending up in a nursing home, 2) making too little food for a party, and 3) losing loved ones.

Only the last fear ever materialized. She lost too many to count. Parents, siblings, children. Some to natural causes, but more to tragic, unnatural causes far before their time. These losses taught her to cherish the time we do get, to enjoy every moment and every bite.

Like any good grandma, she constantly fed people. Not just her own grandkids—this was a woman who brought baked goods TO THE GYM to feed the personal trainers, in flagrant disregard for their low-carb diets. (For years she went regularly for water aerobics and socializing.)

Babushka lived with her heart wide open. There was no such thing as a stranger. Everyone was family. Connecting with people was as natural and vital as breathing.

At the start of the pandemic, upon hearing that large gatherings were being banned, she joked with my mom, "Well, I definitely can't die this year—I want a big festive funeral!"

She died early the following year, after two painful hospitalizations, despite my family's best efforts to shield her from the virus. We had to wait several months to gather loved ones from around the country for a memorial service. It was big but only somewhat festive. Her absence left a gaping hole.

Babushka's favorite pastime was to make people feel not simply loved, but fully worthy of love. Compliments came standard and often.

> *See the light in others, and treat them as if that is all you see.* —Wayne Dyer

That is how she treated us. It was almost comical, how she didn't see our faults, only our strengths. To her love wasn't optional. Giving and receiving it was the whole darn point of life.

I began writing this piece right after she passed, but the grief was too raw. After some time to process, I am ready to share my favorite bits of wisdom from an extraordinary woman.

ALLA POLSKY

One day you will miss these seemingly hard times

My Babushka did not have an easy life. She was six when the Nazis invaded, her Jewish family pulled apart. Some of her survival stories during the war years blow my mind.

The post-war years were hard in other ways, but she always recalled them with a hint of nostalgia, not simply with pain. I asked her why once. "Yes, life was very hard, but also very *interesting*," she emphasized. "There were always people around, so many of us squeezed into one house." She seemed to even miss the daily dramas, the noise, the lack of privacy.

It made me realize that even in the darkest times, you can always find something to be grateful for. Those little daily moments that seem so ordinary today—a call from a parent, a cappuccino with a friend—will one day be the moments you'd give anything to relive again.

Celebrate everything

Babushka grew up during a war, her thoughts occupied with survival, not celebration. After that, she seized any cause for celebration throughout the rest of her life.

For the obvious special occasions like holidays, birthdays, and anniversaries, our home would be filled with decorations, giant stuffed animals, and enough helium balloons to lift a house. But Babushka never missed an opportunity to celebrate the small things in between. Like if my cousin got a new job, she would throw a dinner party with his favorite foods. On my visits home from college, every few months for four years, she insisted on greeting me at the airport with flowers, balloons, and tears of joy streaming down her face. Bystanders must have thought I was returning home from a war zone. No matter how many times I begged her not to make a scene for a routine visit, she made a scene every time. To her it wasn't just a routine visit. She literally counted down the days to each one.

If Babushka met you only once, she would track down your number from a mutual friend and call you on your birthday.

The good news is that we don't need to experience grave hardships like she did in order to appreciate life's little presents. We can skip right to the party.

Don't obsess about beauty

Her entire life, nearly 86 years, Babushka didn't wear an ounce of makeup nor color her hair. Okay, it helped that she was striking without it. Piercing blue eyes, luminous long hair, and an inner confidence that can't be learned in a makeup tutorial.

But even as she aged, gained weight, got wrinkles, went fully gray and then fully white, her appearance was never a source of insecurity or scrutiny. I don't think I ever once saw her looking in a mirror.

"Your grandfather told me I was naturally beautiful and that he far preferred my real face and hair to anything made up," she reminded us anytime we offered her lipstick. He left her a widow in her mid-50s. And though she lived another thirty years without his gaze, she kept on respecting his preference.

I'm not saying that enhancing our appearance with makeup or even surgery is bad. Merely that we are more beautiful when we're not busy fretting about how we look.

ALLA POLSKY

Babushka was a natural beauty, but she made that the least interesting thing about her. Usually she was too busy being interested in everyone else's business.

Be interested

Yenta is a Yiddish word for a nosy busybody who gossips for a living and often (thinks she) has a knack for matchmaking. If you look up Yenta in a Yiddish dictionary, there is probably a picture of my Babushka.

Yes, she was constantly inquiring about our personal lives, our love lives, even our friends' love lives. Yes, I would occasionally get a call or email from a random guy she decided I should meet. Yes, there was that one time she asked me to mail a lock of my hair to a psychic woman in Brooklyn who claimed she could lift the (alleged) curse that had been levied on my love life—presumably the cause of my extended singledom.

No, my grandma wasn't always helpful. But she was always interested. And that intention, that genuine caring for my happiness, is something I wouldn't even trade for a well-lifted curse. Sure, there's a line between being caring and pushy. She crossed the pushy line with so much earnest, well-meaning hilarity that you didn't even care.

The lesson I learned from my grandma here: make your loved ones feel like their lives deeply matter to you. Don't stick to safe small talk. Ask the personal questions because you care. (But don't send money or hair to so-called psychics in Brooklyn.)

Be fearless enough to help

LOST & FOUND

On the 'fight or flight' spectrum, my grandma was a fighter. She didn't think, she just took action. It wasn't always a winning strategy, but it taught me a lot about courage.

When I was 12, she walked my sister and me home from school only to find our neighbor's house on fire. Not a little smoke, but a four-alarm, roof-ablaze movie fire. Babushka immediately grabbed the water hose from our backyard, extended it as far as it would go, and started spraying the flames. I think she told me to go inside and call 911, but all I really remember is how she didn't hesitate to help. A moment later we heard the fire truck siren. I'm pretty sure she didn't drop the hose until they made her.

No one is completely fearless. A little fear can be useful, while too much fear can paralyze you from doing good things. I am grateful I had a role model who was a fighter, to balance out my natural tendency for flight and freeze.

Medicine lies on a plate

This expression sounds even more pithy and elegant in Russian. It's no big secret today that food can be a source of health or illness, depending what's on your plate. But it's a lesson my grandma learned far too late. A lesson she taught me by doing the opposite.

After a lifelong diet of fried food and sweets, coupled with an aversion to exercise, she spent the last two decades of her life in chronic pain—with a smorgasbord of preventable ailments like diabetes, high blood pressure, vertigo, headaches, nausea, losing most of her teeth. (Some of these were likely side effects of necessary medication.)

ALLA POLSKY

Her mind was still razor-sharp in her eighties, but her body made her suffer on every level. This is a courtesy reminder to take care of yours now so you can enjoy it later. Much later.

Love is the entire point

My grandma unabashedly loved a good love story, both in real life and fiction. By my conservative estimate, she read three romance novels a week for three decades. And as mentioned above, she butted into everyone's love life. But it wasn't only romantic love she valued. It was just plain love.

She started and ended every phone call to family and friends with those three simple words. If it was a lengthy call, she would wedge a few 'I love you's" into the middle, too.

And here's the crazy part. She expected nearly nothing in return. I am ashamed to admit there were times in my life when I was completely absorbed in my own little world. I neglected to call her for weeks, even though I knew it would make her day. But whenever I did call, she reacted with roughly the same level of genuine surprise and gratitude as someone who had just won the Powerball lottery.

She wasn't pretending. Unconditional love was her default setting. This extraordinary woman lived for love, and right before she died, I made her a promise that I would, too.

Afterword

It turns out that living for love is relatively easy and enjoyable. Living in an active construction site, not so much.

Herb and I are currently about three months into a large-scale renovation of the lakefront property we bought in Guatemala. Once completed it will house our own little apartment, our live-in school for up to twelve residents, and a large gathering space for classes, cacao ceremonies, yoga and meditation.

Our three project managers, all optimists, estimate one more month of heavy construction before we have a livable space. Some days I genuinely don't know if I have another month of sanity left, let alone the likely longer span of time.

The last few months have taught me all sorts of fun, new phrases in Spanish, like, "We have no electricity or running water again" and "How could a septic tank possibly cost that much?" Every day is a game of utilities roulette. What will be accidentally shut off today—water, electricity, or internet? Some days it's all three, and those are the days I suspect the universe is really testing me. *How badly do you want this new life?* This new spiritual center and year-long course that you and Herb have ambitiously decided to build in 120 days?

ALLA POLSKY

Deep down I know it's not even a choice. We are doing this massive thing—putting in the work, the money, the energy—but on a deeper level we are not in control. It's a force that feels bigger than us. And probably by no coincidence, it's the culmination of everything we have learned how to do over the years, channeled toward something that will hopefully help a lot of people.

Panic attacks. Before we broke ground on construction a few months ago, I had only ever experienced one where I couldn't breathe, rather inconveniently while scuba diving a hundred feet underwater. Now suddenly another half dozen notches have been added to my panic attack record. Externally there is no shortage of obvious causes and stressors. The constant noise from twenty construction workers demolishing old walls and putting up new ones. The consequent living situation that has us squatting in the least disheveled bedrooms. The gangs of street dogs barking and growling at me on my own front lawn—we have no fences for security yet. The large sums of money Herb and I have invested in this building project.

Right now life feels so turbulent and uncertain on the surface. Yet somewhere deep within, my inner knowing, that little voice we call intuition, is whispering, "Don't worry. Every little thing is gonna be alright." My intuition doesn't sound exactly like Bob Marley, but that's the gist of it. Somehow, inexplicably, against the logic of my rational mind and the reality of my bank account balance, I know that this is going to turn out marvelously. I am finally allowing myself to trust that calm reggae voice residing in my heart instead of the nervous squirrel that lives inside my head.

Herb and I celebrated our two year anniversary last week. In some ways it feels like we have been together for two lifetimes, and in a lot of ways we are just getting started. I remind him in between panic attacks and suddenly severe allergies that I would not be doing ANY of this without him. I would be lying on a beach somewhere, or diving for megalodon fossils. I would not be hyperventilating on a broken toilet, nor expelling seemingly infinite stockpiles of snot into Guatemalan tissues that make sandpaper feel like silk.

But then I would also be forfeiting this completely illogical sense of calm and contentment lodged deep in my core. When we stand together on top of the rubble where our new home will be, after the workers have left for the day and the place is quiet, there is magic in the air. We both know it. Whoever said that the right path was going to be silky smooth and free of power outages? We have no choice but to surrender to the unique chaos of living in a construction site. At least for another month, at which point it shall morph into the unique chaos of running a yearlong live-in course on hypnotherapy, meditation, NLP, EFT, lucid dreaming and cacao as a plant medicine.

Part of the magic we both sense in the air might be coming from our next door neighbors: Keith (the Chocolate Shaman you met in Chapter 9) and his life partner, Barbara. If the universe has a sense of humor, it manifests most hilariously in real estate. Herb and I first met on Keith and Barbara's porch, about four years before we returned to San Marcos and bought the property that would have us living literally a few yoga mat lengths away from the porch where we first laid eyes on each other. We go on double dates with Keith and Barbara now. They proudly take credit for the cosmic assist on our relationship while I quip that there's a new 'chocolate power couple' in town.

Upon witnessing one of my allergy attacks, Keith explains that allergies are often a manifestation of *fear* coming out in the physical body. It makes complete sense. I've been having a severe allergic reaction to the fear of failure. This immense building project and creation of a brand new healing center is one of the scariest things I have ever done. It's also one of the most meaningful.

This is what I wished for, after all. A life filled with love and purpose, the two inextricably linked. My business partner and life partner being the same extraordinary person.

My sister read a draft of this book and said, "I think you might be bragging about your relationship too much."

I share my personal story (another scary, vulnerable move) not to brag but to give renewed hope to anyone else who might be losing theirs. Finding love and purpose and happiness and even enlightenment are so freaking possible. Even when they feel far away. Especially when they feel far away.

A few weeks ago I woke up with allergies and sinus pressure (and presumably fear) so physically painful that I started sobbing in bed. With genuine concern Herb asked, "What can I do?"

LOST & FOUND

"Please just leave me here," I said. I didn't want him to see this sad, weak, broken version of me yet again. Lately there had been a streak of more Sad Alla days than happy ones.

But Herb didn't leave. Instead he hugged me so supportively tight that it made me cry even harder and longer than I had in a long time. "I'm sorry I'm such a mess," I sputtered. He replied with quite possibly the kindest, most helpful words ever uttered by a boyfriend. "I would always rather have a bad day with you than a great day without you."

Herb happens to be a terrible liar, so I know he meant it. I also know that we will have many great days, and undoubtedly some bad days, together. I've had plenty of each on my own, too. Love doesn't shield us from pain. It only means there is someone around to bear-hug us indefinitely, without needing us to change, until we resume believing that every little thing is going to be alright.

Acknowledgements

This book would not exist without the intellectual guidance and emotional support of my family, friends, mentors, and spirit guides. I want to thank Keith Wilson and Barbara Gitlin for being kind enough to open their porch to thousands of soul-seekers over more than a decade of cacao ceremonies.

Immense gratitude goes out to my fellow world travelers for their friendship and writing inspiration. Especially Tanaya Lambert, who turned me into a diver and altered the course of my life. Special thanks to Kerin Morrison, Tim Maleeny, and Evan Slater for keeping me in the New York agency world by being irresistible to work with and learn from. They made me a better writer and storyteller. To Marianne Wells for making me a really real yoga teacher. To Angela Bates for channeling life wisdom constantly and constructive edits occasionally.

To my family, infinite thanks for being my first readers and cheerleaders, and for being the type of loving, stable, supportive family that would bore a psychotherapist. To my Black Lotus crew, big thanks for keeping me motivated to finish this book and for calling B.S. on my excuses along the way. To Herb, thank you for just about everything.

1. Jung, Carl. Synchronicity: An Acausal Connecting Principle. Bollingen, CH: Bollingen Foundation, 1952.

2. Campbell, Frances. "Synchronicity". In Leeming, D.A. ; Madden, K.; Marlan, S. (eds.). Encyclopedia of Psychology and Religion. Boston, MA: Springer, 2010. 888–889.

3. Epstein, David. Range: Why Generalists Triumph In A Specialized World. Riverhead Books, New York, 2019.

4. Schwartz, Barry. The Paradox of Choice. Harper Perennial: New York, United States, 2004.

5. Tuk, Mirjam A. and Trampe, Debra and Warlop, Luk, "Inhibitory Spillover: Increased Urination Urgency Facilitates Impulse Control in Unrelated Domains." 2010.

6. Choquette, Sonia. "Sonia Choquette on Intuition as the Key to an Amazing Life." Inspired Evolution Episode with Amrit Sandhu, 2020.

7. Choquette, Sonia. "Sonia Choquette on Intuition as the Key to an Amazing Life." Inspired Evolution Episode with Amrit Sandhu, 2020.

8. Brylske, A. Encyclopedia of Recreational Diving (3rd ed .). Professional Association of Diving Instructors, United States, 2006.

9. Miller, Lisa. "Depression and spiritual awakening: two sides of one door." TEDx Talks, TEDxTeachersCollege, 2014.

10. Lowry CA, et al. "Identification of an immune-responsive mesolimbocortical serotonergic system: Potential role in regulation of emotional behavior." Neuroscience, 2007.

11. Kobayashi, Kenji and Hsu, Ming. "Common neural code for reward and information value." Published in PNAS, 2019.

12. Taruffi, Liila and Koelsch, Stefan. "The Paradox of Music-Evoked Sadness: An Online Survey." Published in PLOS ONE, 2014.

13. Joel, Samantha and Eastwick, Paul W. and Allison, Colleen J. and Wolf, Scott. "Machine learning uncovers the most robust self-report predictors of relationship quality across 43 longitudinal couples studies." Published in PNAS, 2020.

14. Szabo, Arthur. Professor of Psychology, University of Kiel. A two-year study of working professionals in West Germany, 1980s.

15. Mauss, Iris B. and Tamir, Maya and Anderson, Craig L. and Savino, Nicole S. "Can Seeking Happiness Make People Happy? Paradoxical Effects of Valuing Happiness." Emotion, 2011.

16. Gilbert, Daniel. Stumbling on Happiness. Knopf: United States and Canada, 2006.

17. Liudmila Titova & Kennon M. Sheldon. "Happiness comes from trying to make others feel good, rather than oneself." The Journal of Positive Psychology, 17(3), 2022. 341-355.

18. Brickman, P. and Coates, D. and Janoff-Bulman, R. "Lottery winners and accident victims: Is happiness relative?" Journal of Personality and Social Psychology, 36(8), 1978. 917-927.

19. Fredrickson, B.L. and Cohn, M.A. and Coffey, K.A. and Pek, J. and Finkel, S.M. Open hearts build lives: Positive emotions, induced through loving-kindness meditation, build consequential personal resources. Journal of Personality and Social Psychology, 95(5), 2008. 1045-1062.

20. Killingsworth, Matthew. Track Your Happiness.org Project. Harvard University.

21. Williams, Alex. "Can You Poison Your Way to Good Health?" The New York Times, 2021.

22. The 14th Dalai Lama. Stril-Rever, Sofia (compiled by). My Spiritual Journey: Personal Reflections, Teachings, and Talks. HarperCollins, 2009.

23. Kahn, Matt. "Soul Contracts, Twin Flames & Soulmates Redefined." YouTube video, 2015.

24. Sutcliffe, William. Are You Experienced? Hamish Hamilton, 1997.

Made in the USA
Coppell, TX
22 August 2023